Issues in Women's Development

Issues in Women's Development

Anjali Kurane

RAWAT PUBLICATIONS
Jaipur • New Delhi • Bangalore • Hyderabad • Guwahati

ISBN 978-81-316-0520-2

Published by
Prem Rawat for **Rawat Publications**
Satyam Apts, Sector 3, Jawahar Nagar, Jaipur 302 004 (India)
Phone: 0141 265 1748/7006 Fax: 0141 265 1748
E-mail: info@rawatbooks.com
Website: www.rawatbooks.com

New Delhi Office
4858/24, Ansari Road, Daryaganj, New Delhi 110 002
Phone: 011 2326 3290

Also at *Bangalore, Hyderabad* and *Guwahati*

Typeset by Rawat Computers, Jaipur
Printed at Nice Printing Press, New Delhi

Contents

Acknowledgements vii

1 **Indian Women in Development Perspective** **1**
Designing Development for Women in India 3
Issues Involved in Women's Development 6
The Study 14

2 **Socio-Cultural Issues** **25**
Decision-making among Women 25
Role Fluidity between Husband and Wife or Male and Female 73
Attitude Towards Property Rights of Women 90

3 **Educational and Economic Issues** **95**
Educational Issues in Women's Development 95
Economic Issues in Women's Development 114

4 **Mass Media and Political Issues** **149**
Role of the Mass Media in Women's Development 149
Political Issues in Women's Development 168

5 **Case Studies** **187**

6 **Summary and Conclusion** **197**

Bibliography 221
Index 227

Acknowledgements

This book is the result of my work and interest in women-related issues. I owe my sincere gratitude to Board of College and University Development (BCUD), University of Pune, Pune, for providing grant to conduct the present research on the issues involved in women's development.

I am extremely grateful to Mrs Jyoti Shetty who has worked as field investigator as well as research assistant in this project. Her sincere hard work enabled me to successfully complete this research work. She was the backbone of this project.

I am also grateful to Mr Shantanu Ozarkar, Lecturer, Department of Anthropology, University of Pune, Pune, for his support during the compiling stage of the project.

I also express my thanks to Mr Shinde, Mr Waghmare and Mr Kamble, the non-teaching staff of Anthropology Department, University of Pune, Pune, for their co-operation and help throughout this study.

I specially thank all my respondents who gave their valuable time, shared their experiences and provided necessary and valuable information for the present study.

I am also thankful to my brothers Aakash and Ashish for their valuable support throughout the research and my sister-in-law, Nirmala, for her help during fieldwork.

Finally, I am deeply indebted to my mother, whose love, care, and support made this study fruitful.

1

Indian Women in Development Perspective

To live with dignity all the time is the fundamental right of all human beings. The UN General Assembly adopted the Declaration on Rights to Development in 1986. The Declaration defines development as a comprehensive economic, social, cultural and political process, which aims at the improvement of all individuals on the basis of their active, free and meaningful participation in development and the distribution of benefits from development fairly to everyone. The World Bank looks at development as a process that ends with freedom from poverty and from other socio-economic deprivations.

Development is a human-centred process. A prerequisite for development is participation of all people in building their society, it is the privilege of all people to enjoy the benefits of this participation in common efforts. People are the ends as well as the means in this process.

Development is multidimensional, total and both qualitative and quantitative in nature that entails social, economic, political, material, legal, administrative, psychological and cultural values on which the full development of human behaviour and self-respect of man in the society depends. It is a value-laden concept that improves socio-cultural, economic, material and non-material well-being of the society.

The word 'development', therefore, connotes material progress at one end and social and economic liberation at another end. So everyone seems to have their own meaning of development. Though there are different views on the concept of development, it is seen that development is essential and everybody wants it. Therefore, to understand development one should see it from several angles.

Development for common person means provision for basic needs like food, clothing and shelter and some guarantee for stability in life. The dictionary meaning of development is gradual evolution or completion. L.P. Vidyarthi (1981) says, "development means growth plus change" that involves both material and human factors. According to R.P. Misra (1985), development means increase in material and social welfare through increase in productivity, education, health, freedom, safety, opportunity, participation in national, regional and local affairs, rich family life, community feeling, art, music and so on. For instance, it would be a piece of land and a pair of bulls to till the land for a poor landless agricultural labourer, a piece of bread for a hungry man, employment for an unemployed youth, two cars for a person having one car. Anjali Kurane (2005) says, "development means increase in material wealth through productivity, increase in social well-being through education, health, improvement in social content of the human life, community feeling, music, art, safety, freedom, opportunity, sense of participation in local, regional and national affairs, depending on the individual interest and preferences".

Development is broadly understood as growth of human capabilities for acquiring control over natural forces and processes with the aim of improving the material basis of human life. In the modern age, man's power over nature due to advancement in scientific knowledge and technology has resulted in growth of material goods and services, especially in the developed countries. But development in the wider sense means much more than the growth of material wealth, it also means utilizing material wealth as a means of achieving non-material ends for improving the quality of life. In other words, growth should be a means of enriching the lives of everyone, it should serve as an aid to liberation, especially for women, from all forms of social and economic exploitation.

Development, in any country, means the improvement in the quality of life of the people as a whole as also of the individual. A nation's development is determined by its economic, social and technological development.

Designing Development for Women in India

Designing for development involves evaluating the needs of the people in the society, discarding some old traditions, customs, practices and manners and creating some new socio-cultural values and attitudes towards women by introducing structural changes and making new institutions which not only serve a few individuals or groups but promote all sections of the society and involve people in the decision-making processes.

It is a known fact that women form the most vulnerable section of the society. They remain backward educationally, economically and socially. Lalitha K. Sami and Shahida (2001), in their study quoted Amartya Sen, who observes, "seven types of inequalities the women often suffer from such as mortality inequality, natality inequality, basic facility inequality, special opportunity inequality, professional inequality, ownership inequality and household inequality. Over time he feels that the country can move from one type of gender equality to other forms of that inequality. For example, the skewed sex ratio in our country shows the anti-female attitudes of the society. He explains the concept of development as 'freedom of choice' and as a process of expanding the real freedoms that people enjoy. It includes freedom to participate in the economy, freedom of political expression and participation, social opportunities, transparency guarantees, and protective security guaranteed by social safety nets, such as unemployment insurance or famine relief".

In order to understand the issues involved in women's development one needs to know the historical perspective of women's development. According to the historians, the early Vedic period women had the same educational and social opportunities as men. They enjoyed a position of high status and respect. Ram Ahuja (1994) points that in Vedic period, Indian women had ample rights and were not treated as inferior or subordinate but equal to men. The status of women was lowered in the 'Pauranic' period, pre-puberty marriages came to be practised, widow remarriage was prohibited, education was denied to women, sati and 'purdah' system came to be practised, and property rights were denied to them and so on. Women in the Buddhist period had an honourable place in social field but their political and economic status remained unchanged. From the first invasion of India by the Muslims till the middle of the eighteenth century, when the British established their rule in the country, women continued to hold low status in the society. According to Padmini Sengupta (1974), Muslim period was regarded as the black period in the history of women when status of women in India was at its lowest ebb. During the British rule, a number of changes were made in the economic and social structure of our society and some progress was achieved in eliminating inequalities between men and women due to industrialization and spread of education through the Christian missionaries. In the end of the nineteenth century, women in India suffered from disabilities like child marriage, severe restrictions on widows, non-access to education and restricting oneself to domestic and child-rearing functions. The social movements initiated by social reformers such as Raja Ram Mohan Roy, Swami Vivekanand, Jyotiba Phule, Maharshi Karve, Swami Dayanand Saraswati played an important role for equal rights of women and as such these movements succeeded in arousing social consciousness for the liberation and equal status of women.

Today, though there are a number of legislative measures for improving women's status, women still suffer and gender discrimination is an all pervading form of institutionalized deprivation. P. Thomas (1964: 306) says, "In free India Government is trying its best to provide equal opportunity in social, economic and political fields and several efforts are being made to develop women". Yet social outlook and patriarch psyche of men have not changed and women are in the subordinate position in the society. The traditionally defined sex roles, socio-cultural values and attitudes, various customs and practices prevalent in Indian society hamper women's access to education and employment. In Indian culture, women's role is of self-sacrifice and tolerance. Razia M. Parvin (2005) states that though women constitute half of any country's human endowment, they are brought up in the culture of silence. Women continue to be exploited and marginalized in each and every walk of life such as food, health, education, economy and political participation and suffer from lack of fundamental needs and amenities. As women are oppressed, depressed, exploited, underprivileged and being the weaker section, they need social and economic protection. Adequate access to resources, power and decision-making is a must towards gender justice. Gender equality and development of women are recognized globally as the key elements to achieve progress in all areas as women represent half the human resources and half the potential in all the societies. Efforts to promote gender equality between men and women can contribute to the overall development of human society and the nation's progress. Swami Vivekananda said: "... a nation would not march forward if women are left behind."

Despite successive decades of activism, number of movements, legislation, policies and programmes and the developmental efforts at improving the status of women but women in India continue to suffer social and physical cruelties. Although some significant improvements have been observed in expectancy of life and literacy rates among women, they still remain a vulnerable section of the society. The literacy gap between men and women is large. The labour market is not open to men and women alike. In spite of measures to remove the practice of dowry – more deaths are occurring due to dowry demands, more cruelties are inflicted on women. There has been no breakthrough in women's participation in the decision-making process.

The world in general and particularly in the developing countries have identified women's development as one of the thrust areas as they are facing numerous problems related to the issues involved in women's development.

Women constitute half of the country's population, in other words half of the country's human resources. No country can achieve the goal of development without taking into account the gender factor. This was clearly indicated in HDI (Human Development Index) 1995 that women all over the world are receiving unequal treatments. The perspective of women and development is not only important because they comprise of almost 50 per cent of the population but it needs to be discussed as they are the most deprived section in any community due to several reasons and patriarchy is one of the dominating reasons. Equality of women is needed not just on the grounds of social justice but as a basic condition for social, economic and political development of the nation. Recent decades have witnessed a critical emphasis on increasing role of women in the socio-economic development of the country.

Therefore, the need to provide a special thrust to the development of women in order to have an integrated socio-economic development of the country has been felt from the beginning of the planning period in the country. The five-year plans placed special emphasis on providing minimum health facilities, integrated with family welfare and nutrition for women and children, acceleration of women's education and their representation in labour force. A number of laws such as Equal Remuneration Act of 1976, The Dowry Prohibition Act of 1961, The Hindu Succession Act of 1965, The Maternity Benefits Act of 1961 and many more have been enacted for the benefit of women.

For the present study, in order to understand the issues involved in women's development, I have prepared the following operational definition of development. Development means growth of human capabilities and freedom and meaningful participation in each and every aspect of life. For instance, meaningful participation in decision-making process at family as well as society level, freedom to have choice and opportunities in socio-cultural, educational, economic and political spheres of life and freedom from domination, exploitation and economic dependence.

Issues Involved in Women's Development

There are many important issues involved in women's development and which are responsible for the low status of women such as socio-cultural, educational, economic, role of media and participation in the politics.

Socio-cultural

In the Indian society, women's role traditionally has been of childbearing and homemaking while men performed outside activities and earned for the family. This arrangement served our society admirably for centuries. In social ladder, women are at the lowest rung, in the economic field they are the poorest, in education they have the lowest percentage of literacy and in politics also they are lowest in percentage. The patriarchal nature of the Indian society aggravates women's problems and they have to suffer due to gender-biased attitudes of the society in all spheres of life. Since ancient times women have not been able to get their rightful place in society and as citizens in the mainstream of society.

The inequality and subordination of women is an important feature of the Indian social system. Gender discrimination has its roots in history and culture, and is multidimensional in nature. Girls are prepared and socialized right from childhood not to mix up with boys, they are restricted to move alone, sometimes they are restricted in the pattern of dressing also, they do not have freedom in selecting their partner, they are not involved in any decision-making. In the past, marriage was considered an important event in a woman's life, a girl who did not marry was looked down upon with suspicion. Women are conditioned to revere father and to serve the husband as a devotee serves God. The concept of 'pativrata' is present in all religions but it is particularly idealized and firmly institutionalized in the Hindu religion. The term 'pativrata' connotes a wife who has accepted service and devotion to the husband and his family, as her ultimate religion and duty. Consciously or unconsciously discriminatory socialization is practised in the Indian society. Keeping in view the requirements of the husband's family in which daughters have to serve, later they are trained as great cooks, good domestic workers with less assertive characters, while a son is encouraged to study in good schools and do professional courses so that he will be an economic asset to the family and his value in the marriage market increases. Daughter's higher education is an increased liability as they have to get her married to equally or better-educated groom with a huge dowry. The daughter becomes a 'paraya dhan' after marriage and is not supposed to look after her parents even if she is an earning member. The daughter is not allowed to perform funeral rights as it is thought that the soul will not attain salvation. Though law has endured equal property rights to a son and a daughter, it is not practised in reality and the daughters do not fight for it legally for fear of spoiling the relationship with the brother and parents.

Also, in the husband-wife relationship, voluntary acceptance of the superiority of the husband is seen. Till today, the husband sits on the chair, wife sits on the mat, wife eats only after serving food to her husband. Here also the husband is served hot food, and he is not given leftover food. The wife accepts her husband as head of the family; his decision is the final decision on any matter. The wife also tolerates his scolding and sometimes even beatings for no fault of hers. She has no right to decide the number of children she will have, and only as a mother of sons she enjoys authority in the household.

Women in the Indian society are traditionally the providers of nutrition to the family and their nutritional profile is also a part of the household's nutritional profile. Meera Chatterjee (1989) points out that while women are in a commanding position over the household resources that determine individual nutrition, they are themselves quite malnourished, often more so than other family members. In many Indian societies, the labour of women is highly exploited in the kitchen room but no importance is given to their diet. They cannot take their food prior to other members. On the other hand, food cannot be thrown out since this would invite the anger of 'Laxmi', the goddess of wealth, so the leftover food is consumed by the females of the house. It is the duty of the females to see that males and especially the husbands must sumptuously and satisfactorily have their meals. Women are considered as secondary and their bodies are perceived as machines for childbearing and rearing, women are targeted for population control, the declining sex ratio is indicative of higher death rates among women. It also suggests the increasing rate of sex selective abortion. The health status of women too reflects this gender bias clearly. Malini Karakal (1991) reports that women's health is neglected in terms of access to food, medical attention during illness and indifference of family members as well as society towards women's health problems. The recent Family Health Survey-II (1999) showed that 51.8 per cent women are anemic. Malnutrition is higher in adolescent girls. Das Gupta (1987), Miller (1981) and Shiva (1982) report that disparities in feeding patterns start from infancy and continue even during adulthood. Thus, it is seen that women suffer from multiple health problems as shorter life expectancy, experience high maternal mortality, and have higher incidence of chronic diseases and conditions such as chronic energy deficiency, nutritional anemia, osteoporosis, diabetes, hypertension and other cardiovascular diseases.

However, Indian society is undergoing a basic metamorphosis. The changing socio-cultural values are gradually cutting the roots of the traditional value system. The introduction of technology, scientific innovations and industrialization have brought sweeping changes into the way of life and the traditional social order of India. These social changes have not left the women untouched and the position of women in the Indian society is clearly in the process of transformation and will have an important impact on the future development.

Today, the role of women goes much beyond the confines of the home, the boundaries of the gender division of labour between productive and reproductive roles are gradually being crossed as the woman is adopting a career of her own and sharing equally with men the responsibility for the development of the country in all aspects.

Educational

Education is the process that liberates mind. It is liberation from all forms of darkness and ignorance. It is a lifelong process of learning and empowerment and is the basis of change and development. Education has been identified as the most important instrument for improving women's position in society all over the world. It develops the personality of the individuals, makes them eligible to fulfil certain political, economic and cultural functions and thereby improves their socio-economic status. In the Programme of Action of the International Conference held in Cairo in 1994, on Population and Development, education was considered as the most important means to empower women with the skills, knowledge and self-confidence necessary to participate fully in the development process.

In Indian society, a girl child is considered as an economic liability and as a 'paraya dhan' (other's property as she goes to other house after marriage). Therefore, the parents are reluctant to spend on her education as she has to be married off with a dowry. In addition to it, more education for the daughter means more dowry and difficulty in finding a suitable partner. Also, the parents cannot rely on her in their old age and she has no economic compulsion as her main duty is to look after the house and family. In rural areas of India, there is reluctance to educate a girl child, as schools are few, far from their houses, or the families cannot afford them or from fear for their safety or they are needed to help in the household and on the farms. Government schools grow in number with no school buildings or classrooms and shortage of teachers and funds. So, the overall picture of women's education is one of limited opportunity with a number of difficulties and questionable quality. Because of illiteracy the process of decision-making is not adequate among women. The male-female literacy gap, which was to the tune of 25 per cent in the 1991 Census, has been reduced to around 20 per cent in 2001. Shiv Kumar Saini (1980: 13–14) reports: "Educational backwardness is a major reason for the women lagging behind. Of the world's one billion illiterate adults, two-thirds are women. Two-thirds of the 150 million children who are not in schools are girls worldwide."

Education is aimed at making women more competent and active units in the process of socio-economic and political development. Therefore, education is an important means to empower women in decision-making in society and to achieve the goals of equality and development.

Economic

Women's economic empowerment is absolutely essential for raising their status in society. Economic development is expected to show a positive impact on women's control over resources and their participation in decision-making. Economic empowerment is the foremost and basic component in the overall development of women. Jasprit Kaur Soni (2006), in her study on women empowerment, quotes Pandit Jawaharlal Nehru, "Freedom depends on the economic conditions even more than political. If a woman is not economically free and self-earning, she will have to depend on her husband or someone else and dependents are never free."

Traditionally, Indian women have a dependency pattern as far as employment is concerned. They were expected to look after the household duties, help in the farms, animal care and handicrafts made at home. Her status as a wife did not give her control over the family income and it was the husband who decided the family expenditure. The participation of women in income-generating activities has been increasing since independence. The economic independence among women not only increases the family income but also helps them to participate more efficiently in household decision-making. But this is possible only if women have full control over their income.

Mira Seth (2001) says that in India though there has been a slight increase in the female work participation rate from 19.7 per cent in 1981 to 25.7 per cent in 2001, this is still much lower than the male work participation rate both in urban and rural areas. It may also be stated that majority of them are concentrated in the unorganized sector where work is irregular, wages are limited and there are hardly any labour rights under the various labour laws. Even in the organized sector the percentage increase of women's employment is more marked in public sector than in the private sector. It is seen that employment in the public sector is highest in Maharashtra and in private sector in Assam followed closely by Kerala. States with low female status have low employment ratios.

Today, even though women are employed and enjoy comforts, they still face many problems. The problems are many from economic to social depending on the level of education, type of jobs, place of work, role conflict and so on. Women working in organized sector face problems like excessive burden of work, official tensions, discrimination from authorities, lack of support from family members and co-workers, time adjustment for official and household work, transport problems, etc. Women working in unorganized sector face problems like difference in wages, long working hours, absence of job security, worsening work conditions, etc. Also, there is a constant feeling of physical insecurity among women who come out to work; this insecurity is bred by a traditional conservative society into women venturing out of their homes to work. It is also seen that women's participation in management jobs remains very low. According to Shahida Lalitha K. Sami (2007), two of the most powerful barriers for women's underrepresentation in executive positions are: (i) behavioural expectations regarding women's role in the family represent a very real obstacle to their corporate upward mobility; and (ii) discrimination in the form of organizational structures and policies.

If women are financially dependent it has a negative effect on their confidence-building. Once women are economically independent they will be able to overcome their dependency on the household as well as society level. Economic empowerment of women is necessary to eliminate poverty. Economically independent women will be a force in political decision-making and development of area. The economic determinants are as important as the political or social determinants in shaping the future of the country.

Role of Media

The ongoing communication revolution has opened up new possibilities for accelerating development, especially for the upliftment of women and children as they form the most vulnerable sections of the society. For propagating the ideas and views regarding employment, health, family planning, education, nutrition, application of science and technology, economic and social development of women and for creating the right type of awareness important instruments of mass media such as radio, television, newspapers, magazines, films, etc., are used. Media, as a vital industry, plays a vital role in initiating opinions on important issues and acts as a catalyst for women's emancipation and empowerment. Various policies and programmes are implemented through the means of mass communication. This is one effective way of development for women.

The content of communication, at any time, indicates the prevailing attitude of the society towards its women. It is seen that the traditional role of women is glorified on television. The woman is portrayed as self-sacrificing, meek, a faithful wife, devoted mother and so on. The average woman is not shown as anything more than a wife, daughter and mother even in films. During the last decade due to woman's movement, films have tried to depict different shades of women's life, but this kind of parallel cinema is patronized by a very small section of the society. The print media generally confines itself to the image of a woman as consumer, glamour-loving, and the wife and in mother's role. Some papers carry special editions on women giving a mix bag of recipes such as tips on beauty, current issues like dowry, rape, sometimes a serious discussion on women's problems but no serious message comes out from these regarding women's status and problems. The advertisement medium also shows the woman cooking, washing and for cosmetics, fabrics and so on she is shown as a sex symbol to sell the products. The female body is used indiscriminately to promote sale of products in ad films, magazines and newspapers.

Since the new role of women is of producers and contributors to the country and this role is not at the expense or exclusion of their traditional role. Therefore, the media's role should be to make/show programmes related to women's present status and image as the status of women is directly related to a country's development.

Level of Political Participation

The status of women can be examined by the level of their political participation, their representation and share in decision-making bodies. The political empowerment of women is one of the most important aspects in the overall empowerment of women. It is seen that political participation of women is very low in decision-making bodies world over. *Herald* (1997) points that women hold just 11.7 per cent of all the seats in parliaments around the world, and only 7.1 per cent are headed by women. There are several reasons for low participation such as cultural socialization which views women as being socialized into feminine and non-competitive roles, division of labour which limits women to domestic sphere, lack of resources like education, employment, lack of skills, political experience, attitudes of the family and society, behavioural codes imposed on women, criminalization of politics, sexual abuse and character assassination – all these hamper women's participation in politics.

But even after six decades of the grant of political equality, statistics over the years reveal that while there is visible gender equality at the voter level, gender visibility within the power structures is a cause for concern. The political participation of women in India is very low. On an average, women's representation in Lok Sabha, from 1952 to 1996, has been 6 per cent and in Rajya Sabha has been 10.3 per cent. The representation of women at state legislative assemblies is also very poor. There exists a large gap between representation and reality. The 73rd and 74th Constitutional Amendments, which have enforced 33 per cent reservation for women in local government, have been an effort to fill in these gaps. It is seen that the women 'panchas' lack an independent power base of their own. As a result, they become dependent on the male members who have been dominating politics for years. Change in the mental attitude and discipline in our administrators, politicians and the system are the only factors which will bring a change in the status of women in India and their development. Effective political participation of women at the local, state and national levels will not only improve the quality and style of governance but will also be a reflection of their needs and eventually their development.

There has been some change in the political, economic and social status of women in the last 50 years, but we can see that the progress is not that satisfactory. A radical change can take place only when the women realize that they themselves possess the power to alter their situation. Reservation will provide them an opportunity to voice their grievances; will equip them to discharge their responsibilities to the best of their abilities. Participation will create more opportunities for women to expand themselves and their personalities and would have a positive impact on the rest of the country. Jasprit Kaur Soni (2006), in her study on women's empowerment, quotes A.D. Benoist's words that, "The highest measure of democracy is neither the 'extent of freedom' nor the 'extent of equality', but rather the highest measure of participation".

Therefore, the present study focuses on the issues regarding the development of women in the areas of socio-cultural, educational, occupational, political and mass media.

The Study

The Problem

The present study concentrates on socio-cultural, educational and economic issues involved in women's development. In addition to it, the study also deals with the women's level of political participation and role of mass media in women's development. In the traditional society, the role of the woman was that of a dependent person confined to her house and family, with no individuality or identity. Major decision-making in important areas rested with the husband or the elder male members. Today, though the Indian society is characterized by persistence and stability of traditions, women's education and employment is playing a pivotal role in bringing changes in the Indian social structure by changing their attitudes towards the institution of family and marriage. The modern educated and employed women have started questioning about their subordinate position and want to have a say in all important issues that concern the family. They are denying following deep-rooted customs and practices regarding mate selection, considering the husband as a God, and performing the traditional duties of women and so on. She is demanding equality and companionship in each aspect of life. Ramanamma (1979) pointed out that modern educated employed women's feeling of equality is seen in the mode of addressing their husbands; on insistence of companionship, decision-making on important matters and control of finance and expenditure. Therefore, the present study, in socio-cultural issues has focused on basic queries such as women's level of participation in decision-making in the family, their attitude towards important decisions of life, freedom of choice, the deep-rooted customs and practices in Indian society, their social participation and property rights. We have also tried to understand the role fluidity accepted and practised in the society. The Fourth World Conference on Women, Beijing (1995) clarifies that women's development cannot carry in isolation. Women are required to be treated as equal partners in development practices and planning.

The history of women's education shows that though the education of women has expanded but is still far from satisfactory. The most striking aspect is the male-female gap in literacy due to discrimination between son and daughter, girls are made to do household work rather than study, absence of any economic compulsion, the dowry problem, the problem of finding a suitable partner, the attitude of considering the girl child as a liability, college or school far from the house are some of the reasons for the slow progress of girls' education. Jasprit Kaur Soni (2006: 70) says, "Education is expected to serve as an indicator of confidence in the strength and solidarity and bring in more development. It helps in development of human personality, social mobility, occupational change and rise of professional, political and social awareness. Education also increases the degree of participation, which is the key to development. It lays the foundation for better decision-making and communication". So, the present study has focused on the educational issues involved in women's development.

Economic empowerment and social awareness are the two important avenues for the social development of women. Economic independence has given the women a self-satisfaction, identity and financial security. But, the work participation of women is strongly influenced by the socio-biological processes and problems such as excessive burden of work, official tensions, discrimination from authorities and non-cooperation from family members. The constant feeling of physical insecurity among women who come out to work is due to traditional attitudes prevalent in the society. It is also seen that women's participation in management jobs is very low. Mira Seth (2001) points out that women's economic empowerment is absolutely essential for raising their status in society as women's employment leads to better education, health and skill development of the family and certainly better opportunities for the girl child. And that would, directly or indirectly, link to the development of a country. Therefore, the present study also inquires the economic issues involved in women's development.

Media plays an important role in directing large-scale social change. It can shape the attitudes and beliefs of people. But generally it is seen that the media confines itself to the image of a woman as consumer. Some papers carry issues on beauty tips, dowry, rape and discussions on women's problems but nothing serious comes out from these regarding women's status and problems. The advertisement medium also shows the woman cooking, washing and for cosmetics, fabrics and so on. She is shown as a sex symbol to sell products in ad films, magazines and newspapers. Here, M.K. Widge and R. Nag (1989) recommend restructuring of content in various media to remove stereotyped images of women. They point out that many social problems are linked with traditional attitudes, beliefs and prejudices against females which continue to exist. So, there is an urgent need to develop suitable mass media strategies for educating and motivating the people.

Therefore, the present study also questions the role of media responsible for women's development.

It is seen that equality of sexes has not been achieved in the political field. Though women voters are increasing in number, tradition still has a strong hold when it comes to active real participation in politics. Reasons such as domestic duties, restrictions imposed by family members, traditional values, increasing use of muscle power and money in politics, lack of interest are hindrances in their political participation. Though women have entered politics through 33 per cent reservation, it is seen that they are a puppet in this male-dominated domain and all the decisions are made by men. Seema Salgoankar (2006) reports that today a strong opinion is building up in favour of increasing women's involvement in the decision-making processes of the government. They need to be involved in the problems of national development. They should achieve the desired goals of equality and opportunity with men and participation in developmental programmes in order to make their full contribution in the larger areas of peace and development. Therefore, the present study inquires on the level of political participation of women.

Significance of the Study

In a developing country like India women are the most important national resources of development as half of our human resources are women. In the Fourth World Conference on Women, it has been noted that women's development should be considered as a necessary part in every aspect of development and not merely as social development. Women's participation in the development is seen as important key to development. Women are voiceless, still suppressed and deprived from their legal rights and duties. It is only through studying them that the social, cultural, economic, educational and technological development can be achieved by knowing the deficiencies and taking necessary corrective actions. The importance of women's development studies is of significance in bringing women to the path of all-round development which will ultimately lead to the country's development. Development of women is necessary not merely on the grounds of social justice but as a basic condition for social, economic and political development of nation. At present, India is going through a transitional phase. There is persistence and stability of traditions, customs and beliefs on one hand and at the same time the status of women, their attitude towards family, marriage, notion of equality and companionship is changing. Women are asserting and claiming equality with men in all aspects. Therefore, assessment of the issues involved in women's development process is necessary. This study would provide analytical account of the issues involved in women's development in urban settings. It may provide some maladies and help to all those policy makers, development administrators, planners, social workers, non-government organizations who are involved in women's development programmes.

The Setting

The present study was conducted among the Maharashtrian women in Pune city (180° 31' N latitude and 73° 51' E longitude) located in the state of Maharashtra situated at the foothills of Sahyadri Mountains. Prior to independence, Pune was predominantly a cultural, educational, administrative and military centre. Pune is known as the queen of Deccan and the cultural capital of Maharashtra because of its historical, social, cultural, political and educational importance. Pune is also known as "Vidyeche Maherghar" (Hometown of education) and University of Pune is called "Oxford of the East". Pune is a major industrial centre having factories at Pimpri, Chinchwad, Dapodi, Hadapsar and Loni-Urali areas, which are suburbs of Pune and is known as the "Automobile City". Pune has a population of four and a half million and is the eighth largest city in India. Pune represents a fusion of old and new, of the traditional and modern, of quaint *wadas* and glitzy malls. Therefore, Pune was selected as a research area for the study.

The important areas and suburbs of Pune city such as Aundh, Shivajinagar, Kirkee, Pune station, Pimpri, Yerwada, Nigdi, Bhosari and Chinchwad were selected for the study. The selection of these areas was purposive. Firstly, people belonging to different socio-economic strata stay in these areas, secondly, illiterate as well as highly educated people live in these areas and thirdly, there are schools, colleges, factories, municipal corporation offices, private offices, as well as government offices located in these suburbs so women were engaged in various occupations in these areas.

Purposive sampling method was used for the study, where participants were selected with known characteristics.

Method of Data Collection

The relevant data for the present study were collected both from primary and secondary sources. A combination of qualitative and quantitative methods of data collection was used. This combination was purposive as this gives a holistic insight to the research problem and adds to the anthropological understanding of the study and gives an in-depth account of the attitudes, opinions, behaviour of a community or a group, which is being studied.

Quantitative data was collected through pre-tested structured questionnaire and to get the views of the group and feel of the important issues of research, unstructured interview schedules were employed in group interviews. The case study method was also employed for intensive investigation and to understand the complex factors that are operative within a social unit, six case studies were conducted.

The Sample Profile

Age

Out of the total sample, 15.5 per cent of the respondents belong to below 25 years age group; 34 per cent belong to 25–35 years age group; 25.6 per cent belong to 36–44 years age group; 20.8 per cent belong to 45–54 years age group; and 4.1 per cent belong to the age group of 55 years and above. It indicates that we have maximum data and views and attitudes of young and middle-aged women and some data from older women.

Marital status

Majority of the respondents, i.e., 73.1 per cent were married. About 21.3 per cent of the respondents were unmarried. Only 3 per cent of the respondents were widows and 2.5 per cent of the respondents were divorcees.

Age at marriage

Almost half, i.e., 50.8 per cent of the respondents were married in the 18–25 years age group; 18.3 per cent of the respondents were married in the 25–35 years age group; 9.1 per cent of the respondents were married below 18 years of age and a negligible, i.e., 0.5 per cent respondents were married in the 35–45 years age group. The data indicates that maximum number of respondents were married between 18–25 years age group.

Age of husband at marriage

Nearly half, i.e., 44.9 per cent of the respondents were married in the 25–35 years age group; 31.8 per cent of the respondents were married in the 18–25 years age group and 2 per cent of the respondents were married in the 35–45 years age group. The data indicates that maximum numbers of respondents were married between 25–35 years, whereas for women the ideal age is thought to be 18–25 years for getting married as can be seen from the previous data on age at marriage for women.

Length of residence in Pune

In all, 42.4 per cent of the respondents are born and brought up in Pune city, whereas 33.5 per cent of the respondents have been living in the city for more than 20 years. Around 7.6 per cent of the respondents have been living in Pune for less than five years, while 6.1 per cent have been living for 6–10 years, 4.3 per cent for 11–15 years and 6.1 per cent for 16–20 years.

Type of house

Majority, i.e., 64.2 per cent of the respondents lived in flats/blocks. About 20.6 per cent of the respondents possessed bungalows and about 15.2 per cent lived in "chawls".

Ownership of house

Almost 84 per cent of the respondents owned houses and 16 per cent of the respondents lived in rented houses.

Family type

In the present study, 63.2 per cent of the respondents were living in nuclear families and some 36.8 per cent of the respondents were living in joint families. The data reveals that higher percentages of the respondents were living in nuclear families.

Vehicle ownership

About 44.4 per cent of the respondents possessed two-wheelers like scooter or motorcycles, whereas few, i.e., 4.8 per cent possessed four-wheelers, only 1.8 per cent had bicycles. And 32.2 per cent of the respondents had two-wheelers as well as four-wheelers, whereas 16.8 per cent respondents did not possess any vehicle.

Educational status

Close to 1.3 per cent of the respondents were illiterate, while 2.5 per cent were educated up to primary school level, 9.1 per cent up to secondary school level, 8.4 per cent up to matriculation or SSC, 10.9 per cent possessed 12th standard/diploma, certificate or technical education, 5.6 per cent were undergraduates, 32.2 per cent were graduates while 18.5 per cent were postgraduates and 11.4 per cent had professional degrees such as doctors, engineers, lawyers and lecturers. Thus, the sample consists of maximum number of graduates and it was also seen that along with highly educated respondents there were few illiterates also.

Occupational status

Some 20.1 per cent of the respondents were engaged in teaching and clerical jobs, next in order (14%) were of the respondents who were self-employed like taking tuitions, running a beauty parlour, tailoring, etc., and doing household business like selling saris, dress materials, "masalas", pickles, cosmetics and so on. Some (13%) of the respondents were in professional occupations such as doctors, engineers, principals, lawyers and lecturers, whereas 12.9 per cent of the respondents helped their husbands or family in their businesses such as Xerox shop, electrical goods shop, general stores, STD and PCO booth, looking after the office work of the husband, 11.9 per cent worked as government officers, NGO officers and corporators, and only 5.1 per cent worked as domestic servants and peons. The data shows that we have respondents from various categories of jobs, from domestic servants to officers in government service and professionals.

Monthly income of the respondents

Some 18.5 per cent of the respondents' monthly income was below ₹ 5,000, 17.5 per cent of the respondents had monthly income ranging from ₹ 5,000–10,000. About 20.1 per cent of the respondents had a monthly income from ₹ 10,000–15,000, while 13.7 per cent of the respondents had a monthly income from ₹ 15,000–20,000; whereas 5.3 per cent of them had a monthly income from ₹ 20,000–25,000 and only 2.1 per cent of the respondents had an income of ₹ 25,000–30,000 and there were some (22.8%) of the respondents who had no income and belonged to the housewives and students category. Thus, we have respondents from the lower strata to the higher strata in terms of monthly income.

Chapter Scheme

Chapter 1 presents the theoretical introduction of the concept of development, designing development for women in India, issues involved in women's development, the statement of the problem of research, significance of the problem, methodology and sample profile.

Chapter 2 deals with the socio-cultural issues involved in women's development. It is divided into two parts. The first part deals with decision-making among married women which is again subdivided into three sections. The first section deals with the decision-making process in the family. The second section concentrates on the opinions on certain deep-rooted customs and practices in the Indian society. The third section focuses on the women's attitude towards social participation. The second part deals with role fluidity between husband and wife or male and female and also focuses on the property rights of women and whether these rights are used by women in Indian society.

Chapter 3 examines the educational and economic issues involved in women's development. The first section concentrates on the educational issues involved in women's development. It analyzes the nature, type, level and aim of education among the respondents. It also deals with the level of participation of the mother in the child's educational activities, and also on the status of educated women. The second section deals with the economic issues among employed and unemployed women. It examines the reasons of working, discrimination on account of sex, utilization of one's earnings, effect on children, conflicts due to the job in case of employed women and in case of unemployed women it examines the oppositions faced for doing a job, preference for part-time and full-time job and opinion of the respondents on women's employment.

Chapter 4 deals with the role of mass media and politics involved in women's development. The first section focuses on the role of mass media and examines the extent of exposure of the respondents to different mass media such as newspaper, television, films and computers, and their impact on them. The second section concentrates on the political issues and it analyzes the respondents' voting behaviour, level of participation in political activities, attitude towards reservation and their opinions on politics.

Chapter 5 deals with the case studies.

Chapter 6 highlights some of the major findings of the investigation and conclusion.

2

Socio-Cultural Issues

This chapter concentrates on the socio-cultural issues among women's development. It is divided into two parts. The first part deals with the decision-making issues among women. It is further divided into two sections. The first section concentrates on decision-making among married women regarding: (a) women's involvement in the decision-making process in the family; (b) opinion on certain deep-rooted customs and practices in Indian society; and (c) attitude towards social participation. While the second section concentrates on decision-making among unmarried women regarding: (a) freedom in certain things in day-to-day life; (b) involvement in family decisions; and (c) opinion on important decisions of life. As the social issues for married and unmarried women are different, the present study consisted of 73.1 per cent of married women and 21.3 per cent of unmarried women. The second part deals with the role fluidity between husband and wife or male and female and with the property rights for women.

I
Decision-making among Women

Decision-making connotes power and the power to make decision is influenced by a prescribed authority pattern. In a family, rights and responsibilities are distributed in such a way so as to ensure smooth functioning of the family. Max Weber (1946: 180) defines power as, "the chance of a man or a number of men to realize their own will in a communal action even against the resistance of others who are participating in action". Power is evident or displayed in the opportunity to make decisions, which affect the life of the family. In a patriarchal system, the elder males mostly make the decisions. A comprehensive study conducted by Murdock (1949: 8), which examined 250 primitive and historic societies, has brought out the fact that far more societies operated under husband-dominance than under any other system, for example, wife-dominance or equality.

Earlier, the patriarch was the guardian of the family, he had unlimited authority over his wife, sons and daughters. In the traditional Indian society, the male played a major role in the social structure compared to the female. In the family also he automatically became the centre and axis of power in the system. Another factor was the economic dependence of women, which did not allow them to gain a position of authority in the family structure as well as in the social structure. A woman was subordinate to man. She lost her individuality upon getting married and she had to depend on her husband.

Women play a major role in home management and household economy but still they are not free to take decisions in important matters of the family. In the traditional joint family, the eldest male, whether grandfather or father, was recognized as head of the family. The wife of the eldest male member, usually the grandmother, had authority over domestic matters of the household. Iravati Karve (1953) has pointed out that all the male members in the joint family are legally the co-owners of the family property right from the birth while women were excluded from the ownership of property. Final or major decision-making in important areas rested with the husband or the elder male members. Sometimes, if a mother-in-law played a dominant role in the family, she was consulted in decision-making especially about marriages. She was given authority in day-to-day affairs. Revolt against the authority structure in the family was considered a sin.

The major sphere of activities for women was limited to the kitchen, feeding the family and bringing up the children.

Earlier, the process of decision-making was clearly dominated by two factors, i.e., age and sex. Joshi (1973) has observed that the participation of married women in activities outside the home has bought some changes in the roles of husband and wife. The husband needs to participate in shopping for the household things and in rearing of children. Also, with the breaking of the joint family system, women are inclined to participate more in the family decision-making. Today, the woman wants to involve herself in decisions, at least regarding children's education, shopping, budgeting and financial matters. Some of them want to take decisions regarding vital issues such as settling of children's marriage, children's mate selection, dowry matters, etc. A more egalitarian role in decisions is what they seem to ask for. Decision-making for the woman at family level is the power to make decisions regarding the education of children, shopping for major and daily items, financial matters, career, mate selection, dowry, the number of children, the sex of the child and family planning. Kapur (1973) finds out that although working women are allowed to take part in the decision-making process, their decision is not final. She thinks that working women themselves do not want to take part in the decision-making process. Data available in *Women and Men India* (2000: 93) reveals that 9.4 per cent of the women in India are not involved in any decision-making at household level. According to the Beijing Declaration (1995), "Women's empowerment and their full participation on the basis of equality in all spheres of society, including participation in the decision-making process and access to power, are fundamental for the achievement of equality, development and peace".

However, it should be noted that even in the traditional family there is gradual change in the relations of power with time. On the whole, the traditional outlook towards the pattern of roles is changing.

Decision-making among Married Women

Decision-making among married women concentrates on three important aspects of women's daily life such as, firstly, women's involvement in the decision-making process in the family, secondly, women's opinion on certain deep-rooted customs and practices in the Indian society and, thirdly, on women's attitude towards social participation.

Women's Involvement in the Decision-making Process in the Family

In order to assess the recent pattern of power of women and their involvement in the decision-making process in family, the following eleven indicators of decision-making were selected such as:

1. Education of children
2. Control over money matters
3. Shopping for major items like fridge, TV, etc.
4. Kitchen and cooking matters
5. Buying and selling of property or house
6. Visits, picnics or outings
7. Settling of marriage
8. Emergency expenses
9. Shopping for daily items
10. Mate selection
11. Decision on the number of children

Education of children

Education is a means of cultural transmission. Both family and education have one purpose in common, that is, the socialization of the younger generation. A child's education starts in his family at home especially by the mother. In a traditional joint family unit, it was the male head of the family who made all the decisions.

In this context, effort was made to find out whether women were consulted in the education of their children. The data reveals that for majority (62.2%) of the respondents, the chief responsibility of making decisions about the education of children was taken by both husband and wife while for few (3.6%) respondents it was the husband who took the decision and in few (5.6%) of the respondents, it was the wife alone who took decision, while others (3.3%) it was the in-laws who took the decision regarding education of children. For negligible (0.8%) number of the respondents it was the husband's and in-laws' decision, while for the rest (0.5%) of the respondents it was the wife and in-laws who decided about the education of children and for the remaining (0.8%), all of them together took this decision. Other respondents were unmarried (21.3%) or were newly married (2%) with no children.

There is significant change in making decisions regarding the education of children. The data shows that the woman is also involved in the decisions regarding education of children. One interesting point to be noted is that few respondents preferred to take decisions in this matter on their own. Though not all, but among majority of the respondents the woman is now being accepted as a decision-maker in the education of children.

Control over money matters

In the traditional family, each member of the family was dependent for his/her needs upon the male head of the family. The head of the family generally took any financial decision. Women were not allowed to interfere in this matter. But under the changed conditions, the educated housewives are taking over the function of controlling the financial matters of the family. The economic dependence and elimination from power structure over financial matters is clearly responsible for the inferior position of women in family and in society.

Thus, the question regarding the control over financial matters was put to the respondents. In the present study, more than half (54.8%) of the respondents said that both husband and wife managed the financial matters. While it is interesting to note that for some of the respondents (9.4%) it was the husband who controlled the money matters and for few (4.3%) it was the wife alone who made decisions regarding this matter. For some (3%) it was the husband and in-laws who made decisions in this matter and in negligible number (0.8%) number of respondents it was the in-laws who made the decisions, while for rest (4.3%) of the respondents, all of them were involved in decision-making.

Thus, the analysis shows that for more than half of the respondents both husband and wife jointly share the decisions regarding control of money matters and still for few of the respondents it was the husband only who took decisions and in negligible number of respondents, the in-laws took the decision on money matters. Hence, it can be concluded that though there is some change and wife's opinion is taken in financial matters yet in a negligible number of respondents the in-laws still have a hold over financial matters.

Shopping for major items such as fridge, TV, etc.

Under former historical circumstances, the husband's economic and social roles gave him authority automatically. The power to make decisions was influenced by an approved authority pattern and in a patriarchal system; the elder males mostly made the decisions. Under modern conditions, the roles of men and women, particularly in urban areas, have changed so much so that the wife's opinion is also considered important. Education and employment of women has given them independence and increased skill in decision-making about shopping for major items such as fridge, TV, sofa set and so the husband gives weightage to his wife's opinions before taking the final decision. This may be due to democratic change in our ideas. It is the women who look after the house, maintain the house and decorate the house so they have the right to decide on something, which comes into the house.

In the sphere of making major purchases, it is seen that for more than half (59.6%) of the respondents it is the husband and wife who take decisions jointly in this matter. While 6.6 per cent of the respondents reported that it was the husband who made the decisions whereas few other (3%) respondents reported that it was the wife who took decisions in this matter. A small number (1.8%) of the respondents said that the in-laws took the decisions whereas others (4.8%) reported that all the family members together took decisions in the matter of major purchases.

One of the respondents under study, whose husband owned two restaurants said, "My husband is busy in his work, he gives me a certain amount every month and I decide what to buy, I go to the shop, select what I want and purchase right from TV, sofa set, microwave, dining table and even gold, it is me who shops for everything." Another respondent said, "My husband and me always used to argue in the shop over shopping. Nowadays we decide what to buy and he gives me the money. I take my son aged 17 years with me and we do all the shopping."

From the above data, it can be concluded that nowadays in more than 50 per cent of the families it was the husband and wife who were the main decision-makers in shopping for major items in the family, while in few families it was still husband-dominated and in few families it was the wife alone taking decisions while shopping for major items, that can be said to be a recent trend.

Kitchen and cooking matters

The preparation of food, the care of the children, and all the washing, scrubbing, cleaning and sweeping involved in the care of home are mainly thought to be a woman's job. Here, the eldest woman finds her main sphere of authority. She is chiefly responsible for the direction and distribution of work. In traditional families, the chief responsibility of the kitchen remained with the eldest lady of the house and other women assisted her. In the recent modern families, the housewife has to look after the kitchen responsibilities all by herself sometimes assisted by her husband but the final responsibility rests with her so the women have important role in home management.

In the present sample, it is seen that for nearly half (40.4%) of the respondents it is the wife who looked to the kitchen matters. In some (26.9%) of the respondents, both husband and wife did this work. For few (1%) of the respondents, all the members of the family took decisions in kitchen matters and for rest (8.1%) of the respondents the women and the mother-in-law did the kitchen work and cooking.

Thus, the analysis indicates that though there is significant change in cooking and kitchen matters, nearly for half of the respondents, the kitchen management is entirely a wife's duty. For some of the respondents, the husband also shares the kitchen work and can be said to be a recent trend in modern families.

Buying and selling of property or house

In the traditional family, the head of the family usually took money-centred decisions. Each member of the family was dependent for his/her needs upon the male head of the family. The head of the family generally looks any financial decision. Females were not allowed to interfere in this matter. But under the changed conditions, the women are also consulted in these financial matters.

In the present study, nearly half (47.7%) of the respondents said that the husband took decisions in this matter. Whereas for some (19%) of the respondents it was the husband and wife who took decisions jointly and in negligible cases (0.5%) the respondents took decisions on their own, as they had no one to rely upon, in these matters. In few (2%) of the cases, all the family members including the respondents took decisions.

The above analysis points out that there is not much change in making decisions regarding buying and selling of property. It is seen for nearly half of the respondents, man is the central figure of economic power structure in the family. But according to some of the respondents women are also being given weightage in money-centred decisions though the percentage is very small.

Visits, picnics or outings

In the busy stress-filled urban life everybody looks forward to weekends and vacations to get away from the daily grind. Generally, the women are expected to remain involved in household activities. Over a period, housework becomes dull and monotonous and even the women need change and relaxation from the routine work. Generally, all the family members are busy in their daily schedules. Everyone yearns to go for outings when the family can relax and spend time together. Formerly, the woman had to just go along with the family wherever the picnic or outing was decided. But now under changed circumstances, the whole family including the children also sit and decide the place to be visited.

The percentage distribution in decision-making about visits, picnics or outings reveals that both husband and wife made joint decisions according to majority (62.1%) of the respondents, while for few (7.1%) of the respondents it was the husband who made decisions and for (4.8%) of the respondents it was the wife who took decisions while for only one per cent of the respondents all the family members including the respondent took decisions.

The above analysis reveals that for majority of the respondents, the husband and wife shared the decision-making jointly regarding simple decisions such as visits, picnics or outings.

Settling marriage

Marriage is an important event in one's life and decision-making in this matter is equally important and it is usually the one who holds the key position in the family decides on this. Madan (1976) and Kala Rani (1976) noted that a woman as a house-maker hardly has a say in this matter. The situation may be different where the woman makes economic contribution but here also in order to have peace and harmony it is the woman who has to make a compromise because of the importance attached to her role as a mother.

In the present study, it is seen that for nearly half (49%) of the respondents, the chief responsibility regarding settling of marriages was taken by both husband and wife. For some (11.9%) of the respondents, it was the husband who took decisions while in few (2.3%) of the respondents it was the wife who took decisions; for a small number (5.6%) of the respondents it was the in-laws who took decisions and for others (2.8%) all the family members together took decisions in this matter. For some (3.8%) of the respondents the husband and in-laws took decisions regarding marriages.

The analysis reveals that for nearly half of the respondents, the responsibility of settling marriages was shared by the husband and wife but still in some families the decisions regarding marriage settlement was taken by the husband and also the in-laws. So, in the present study, we see that though the percentage is small, the wife is given the right to decide about marriage settlement in the family.

Emergency expenses

Generally, it is seen that in a traditional family the man was the main bread earner of the family and the woman's duty was to look after the house and rear the children. But now women have also started earning and contributing to the running of the household. Even though she is an earning member it is seen that in case of emergency expenses such as hospitalization, wedding, gifting, etc., it is the husband who takes the responsibility of these things.

But, in today's situation, in some families it is the wife who earns more than the husband and she shares the major responsibility in running the house, even in the emergency expenses.

In the present study, it is seen that for nearly half (44.4%) of the respondents both the husband and wife share the emergency expenses and in some (22.8%) of the respondents it is the husband who spends on the emergency expenses. In few (2.8%) of the respondents it is the wife, husband and in-laws who take on the emergency expenses. Again, for few (1%) of the respondents, it is the in-laws, and all of them who spend on emergency expenses. For a negligible number (0.5%) it is the wife and in-laws who take responsibility of emergency expenses.

A significant change seen in the above data is that for nearly half of the respondents both the husband and wife contribute to emergency expenses which was till recently considered to be the duty of the man. On the whole, the traditional outlook towards the pattern of roles is changing.

Shopping for daily items

Ideally, it is the woman who had to make purchases of daily items. She had to make purchases when the provisions were cheap and store them properly for consumption. But today in modern times, the traditional idea about the functions of a woman is undergoing change. Due to participation in work she has to make adjustments between her traditional role in the family and new roles outside the family.

In the present study for some (37%) of the respondents, the responsibility of making daily purchases was on the wife. The husband and wife made the daily purchases for some (29%) of the respondents. Only for a few (1.3%) respondents it was the husband who shopped for daily items and the in-laws also made the daily purchases in case of (3%) the rest of the respondents.

The analysis shows that the major responsibility of making daily purchases was on the wife. But in case of some of the respondents, the husband and wife shared this responsibility jointly. It can be seen that the roles of women are splitting up and a change is occurring as in case of a few of the respondents, the husband is also assisting his wife in shopping for daily items.

Mate selection

In India, it was the parents who arrange marriages. Giri Raj Gupta (1976) pointed out that most of the marriages in India took place with the help of a friend, a relative or a negotiator. The girl and the boy had no say nor did they have the liberty to meet each other before marriage. Though parents and guardians continue to arrange marriages, nowadays it is a practice to involve the concerned boy and girl to exchange their views. Moreover, the educated women are choosing their mates themselves and the working women are very particular in selecting their life partners.

In the present study to explore whether the respondents were consulted in their own marriages the following question was put to them, "In the selection of your partner was it your family who made the choice?" Almost for majority (62.7%) of the respondents it was the male members in the family who made the choice of partner for the respondents, while some (15.9%) of the respondents themselves chose their partners.

The analysis indicates that there is not much change in the practice of mate selection, as for majority of the respondents it was the male members in the family who made the choice of their partners. So, it can be said that women have no important role in mate selection while the men still play a significant role in the arrangement of partners.

Decision on the number of children

As Indian society was male-dominated, women were exploited and deprived in every sphere of life to the extent that they did not have a right to decide the number of children they would like to have. In earlier days, children were thought to be blessings of God so a woman would have number of children with no family planning. Early marriage and large number of pregnancies made the women weak and fragile. The preference for sons over daughters was so much that in some families the woman underwent a number of pregnancies till she gave birth to a son. However, today, due to education, the situation is changing. The idea regarding the son as an asset and a girl as a liability is also undergoing change.

In the present study, more than half (54.1%) of the respondents said that both the husband and wife decided on the number of children and for some (16.2%) of the respondents it was their in-laws who made the decision, while for few (4.3%) of the respondents it was the husband's decision and for few (4.1%) of the respondents it was the wife who decided the number of children she would like to have.

The analysis points out that for more than half of the respondents it was the husband and wife who decided on the number of children they would have, this certainly shows the change in attitudes compared with the earlier days where the woman had no voice in this matter. But one interesting point to be noted here is that still in case of some of the respondents it is the in-laws who decide the number of children the couple should have, which shows that tradition still rules in some of the families.

The data available on the above eleven decisions among the Maharashtrian women in Pune reveals that for majority of the respondents, the decisions regarding education of children, control over money matters, shopping for major items, visits, picnics and outings, the number of children they would have, are taken by both husband and wife. This certainly shows the change in attitudes in comparison to the earlier days where the woman had no voice in these matters. While for nearly half of the respondents, the husband and wife share the responsibility in decisions such as settling marriages and emergency expenses. And when it comes to kitchen, cooking matters and shopping for daily items, for nearly half of the respondents, it is the wife who takes the main responsibility and for a marginal number of the respondents, the husband alone decides. But it is an interesting point to note that for nearly half of the respondents it is the husband who takes decisions in major money-related matters like buying and selling of property, etc. It may be due to the feeling of male superiority and more economic rights to men than women. It is also seen that women have no important role in mate selection while the men still play a significant role in the selection of partners.

Women's Opinion on Certain Deep-rooted Customs and Practices in the Indian Society

Indian history shows that the Indian society has remained in the control of deep-rooted customs, practices, orthodoxies and traditions like the low level of education, rigidity in marriage practices, the traditional bondages of kinship, the dowry system, son preference, family planning practices and so on. In the present century, a number of factors such as the emergence of new socio-economic patterns, changing traditions, evolving concepts of culture, opportunities for education and employment have started changing the attitudes and beliefs towards certain deep-rooted customs and practices in India. When the social situation is changing it is natural that the roles and opinions of women will also reflect the change.

The following ten customs/practices were selected to find out the respondents' opinion on it as these customs and practices are directly related to her decision-making process and her position in the family and society.

1. Marriage or career
2. Freedom to daughter in selection of mate
3. Dowry
4. Ideal number of children
5. Expectation of boy or girl during the first pregnancy
6. Family planning
7. Daughter performing funeral rights
8. Discrimination regarding food compared to brother
9. Having meals after serving all the family members
10. Practice of eating leftover food

Marriage or career

Marriage as a social institution, with its various forms and types, is found throughout the world. In Indian society, marriage has a religious sanction and according to Hindu religion life is incomplete without marriage. Marriage was performed mainly for religious fulfilment, or dharma, rather than for pleasure. The main purpose of marriage was believed to be 'dharma' (performance of duty), 'praja' (begetting progeny), and 'rati' (pleasure). Marriage was considered to be a social duty towards family and community and there was little idea of individualism or individual interests and aspirations. Marriage was an important event for women, because it was the only sacrament a woman was allowed to perform in her lifetime. Unmarried man and woman were considered socially inferior. An unmarried girl was said to bring shame to her family. There are numerous rites and ceremonies, which were to be performed by the husband and wife, which could not be performed by the unmarried man and woman. Hindu marriage is a sacrament and it is considered essential for the woman. K.L. Sharma (2007: 149) points out that marriage is a social duty towards the family and the community, and as such there is little individual interest. However, with the husband and wife have never been equal with regard to their obligations and privileges. The wife had to make sacrifices and adjustments. Today, the situation has undergone a change. The socio-cultural awakening, education, employment and feeling of equality to men among women have weakened the sacred culture of marriage. Today, girls do not feel the necessity to get married, instead they like to focus on their careers and be independent.

Women have been participating in economic activities since ancient times till the present. Women in rural areas have always been working outside their homes. However, in urban areas it was believed that the women of lower strata worked outside the home. Seeking employment outside started from early years of the present century and economic pressure seemed to have caused this situation. A significant change took place after 1947 when India became free and the Constitutional declaration that there should be no discrimination against employment of women. This created opportunity and the employment rate increased particularly among educated and upper caste women. C.A. Hate (1930) points out that there are many factors responsible for this change and socio-economic emancipation is one of the sources.

Several factors such as industrialization, loss of security provided by the joint family, individualization, inability of a single person to earn enough for the family has drawn out the women from their homes to the world outside to study and earn. Until a girl gets married her employment is looked upon as a gap to be filled before marriage. However, a working wife represents the inadequacy of the male members of the family. Traditionally, in elite classes, female employment is not favoured. The advancement of education has motivated many a woman to take up a career. The reasons for taking up employment can be financial and non-financial. Neera Desai (1957) points out that a change has been brought about in the outlook regarding the status of women and their role in society. K.M. Kapadia (1959) points out education and the present economic strains as factors for taking up employment.

In this context, the respondents were asked what according to them was important – career, marriage, career and marriage, only marriage or only career.

In the present study, nearly half (47%) of the respondents said that first one should have a career and then get married whereas some (21.5%) of the respondents reported that one should get married first and then think about career. Other few (7.9%) of the respondents said that both marriage and career are important and both should take place at the right time and age and the rest (2%) said that only marriage is important.

In the present study, a significant change was observed in opinion about marriage or career, earlier only marriage was important as it was related to fulfilment of dharma, but now only 2 per cent of the respondents are focusing on marriage only, while nearly half of the respondents want to settle in a career before marriage as they will have financial independence, more status and confidence in doing things, that is a significant change. In addition to this, few of the respondents hold the opinion that both marriage and career are important. And some said getting married is important first. Thus, it is obvious in the present study that career is also important along with marriage.

Opinion about freedom to daughter in selection of mate

Until recently many women were not consulted in their marriages. The brides used to simply nod their heads to confirm their faith in their parents. It was a custom to show respect towards the elders. The picture has somewhat changed now. Women are gradually realizing that they have their own personalities. Education, social status and economic position is affecting their attitude, social behaviour and opinions towards life patterns. Today, girls want to have a voice in choosing their partners.

In the present study, as we have seen in the section on decision-making among married women, though most of the respondents had no say at the time of their own marriage in selecting their partners, yet nearly half (48%) of the respondents were ready to give freedom to their daughters in selecting their spouses. They said that it was their life and they had a right to decide about their life and as a parent they will be there to guide them. Some (12.9%) of the respondents clearly told that they were not in favour of giving freedom to their daughters in this respect as they are not mature enough to take decisions in this matter. The rest (17.7%) of the respondents were a little rational as they reported they were uncertain in this respect and that it all depended on the situation at that time as some respondents had small daughters and some of them had no children at the time of enquiry.

The analysis indicates that attitudes are changing as nearly half of the respondents were ready to give freedom to their daughters in selection of mate and some of them were rational and said that it depended on the situation; that is a significant change.

Opinion about dowry

Dowry is one of the social evils of the Indian society. The dowry custom, if understood and implemented properly, is not harmful but this custom is being misused and so all problems arise. The word 'dowry' means the property that a girl brings with her at the time of marriage. Hooja (1969: 84) points out that the custom of dowry has been prevalent in society since early period and it is a universal phenomenon. As the bride and groom start a new life after marriage the girl or boy's parents help them by providing household articles. As the daughters were not given an equal share in property, this was substituted by presents during their marriages for the well-being of her future out of pure love and affection. This was optional to the bride's parents and not compulsory. Slowly the practice of offering presents changed into a rigid custom. But, in course of time it has become crude tradition resulting in female infanticides, bride burning and other cruelties. He also observes that ethical and economic reasons were influential in making the custom of dowry rigid. For some, it has become a means of exhibiting one's wealth and social prestige.

The middle-class and the poor who cannot afford to pay the dowry are the sufferers. At the time of marriage, commitments are made to give dowry but later on if they are not fulfilled, the daughters-in-law are troubled and humiliated leading to dowry deaths. A.K. Sur (1973) observes that dowry is most prevalent in upper caste and highly educated communities. K.L. Sharma (2007) points out that the problem of dowry has become a serious evil among the upper castes and middle classes, both in towns and villages.

In the present study, the respondents were asked to give their opinions on dowry. Majority (74.1%) of the respondents had a negative opinion towards dowry. The respondents gave various reasons such as: (1) dowry is the worst custom in society, which is responsible for female feticides and low status of women; (2) woman is equally earning and showing her capabilities in all fields as men then why to give dowry; and (3) the dowry custom should be erased from the family level which will bring a change on society level and would lead to empowerment of women and their development. Only few (4.6%) of the respondents had positive opinion towards dowry. Because the respondents feel that: (1) dowry is our tradition; (2) parents give dowry to the daughters lovingly; and (3) parents and daughters have a status in the in-laws house. The respondents were also asked whether dowry was given at the time of their marriage. Some (33.5%) of the respondents said that dowry was given in their marriage. Nearly half (45.2%) of the respondents said that dowry was not given in their marriages. The respondents who were given dowry were further asked whether the dowry given was in gift form or cash form. In case of some (29.7%) of the respondents dowry was given in the form of gifts and to others (14%) it was given in the cash form. Further they were asked whether dowry was demanded or given happily. Some (14%) of the respondents said it was demanded and some (19.5%) of the respondents said their parents gave it happily.

In the present study, six of the respondents out of which four of them were holding jobs and two of them were housewives said, "One has to follow the custom due to societal pressure even if one doesn't like it". So it is difficult to say whether the attitude and discontinuation of the dowry system will play a significant role in the future.

The above analysis indicates that though the custom of dowry is still a feature of our society in the present study conducted among Maharashtrian women in Pune, three-fourths of the respondents held negative opinions towards the dowry system. It was observed that some of the respondents brought dowry at the time of their marriages. Some got dowry in gift form and some in cash form. In the case of some, dowry was demanded. So again it is difficult to say whether in practice the system of dowry will continue or go away because though the respondents have a negative attitude towards dowry it was not practised during the respondents' marriage.

Opinion on ideal number of children

The desire for a child is natural as it satisfies the social and biological needs of a woman. Children are valued as they continue the family and they serve as agents for maintenance of the family status and wealth. A.S. Altekar (1962: 101) writes, in the Vedic age blessings were given to the married couple to bear ten sons, in the Smriti period the number reduced to seven. At present, this blessing will be looked as a curse. Now people have realized that the number of children is not only the will of God but also the result of the planning of parents. Now everybody wants a small family in which each child will receive good attention. But the desire for a male child, particularly if one has one or more female children is widely prevalent and some families are so obsessed about it that they even resort to abortions. It is seen that the parents desire a male child due to economic and religious reasons. Once they have a male issue they limit the family size, otherwise they continue producing children till they get a male issue. Sometimes the man goes for a second marriage if the first wife cannot give birth to a son. She is humiliated and tortured for not giving birth to a male child. The women did not have any right to decide on the number of children. It was the husband and the family who decided the number of children.

In the present study, the respondents were asked about the ideal number of children a couple should have. Some (28.7%) of the respondents said that a couple should have one girl and one boy and some (31%) of the respondents said that a couple should have two children irrespective of sex, while some (16.8%) of the respondents said that a couple should have only one child, either girl or boy. Few (1.5%) of the respondents wanted only two girls and a negligible number (0.7%) of respondents wanted only two boys.

The above data shows that for more than half of the respondents, the ideal number of children are two as the respondents feel that the children learn sharing, caring and helping and there is less chance of developing selfish and individualistic attitude. They understand the importance of relations of sister and brother. The data also points that some respondents still want one male child out of the two children and a negligible number of the respondents wanted only boys. This choice clearly signifies that there is a preference for male children. Nearly half of the respondents are of the opinion that the sex of the child is not important whether the couple has one child or two children. Few of the respondents wanted only a girl, that is a progressive change.

Expectation of a boy or girl during the first pregnancy

When a woman conceives everyone is happy in the family and they prepare for the arrival of the child. But everyone is anxious about the sex of the child. Traditionally, the people had ways by which they could guess the sex of the child, but today sex determination tests are done to know the sex of the child. Due to these tests female feticides take place thus creating an imbalance in the sex ratio. Although the test has been banned, it is done illegally. India being a patriarchal society the birth of a male child is preferred. Dealing with the importance of the birth of a male child, Ross (1961) points out that a woman's position as a mother of sons gives her authority in the household. Promilla Kapur (1973) points out that parents are not keen to send daughters even to primary schools unlike sons. Vatsala Mehta (1956) writes that the birth of a female child was unwelcome during the ancient days. The son helped the parents in procuring food, hunting animals, protecting the parents from the enemies, looking after them in old age whereas the daughter was of no help; moreover she always had to be guarded for fear of going astray. After marriage, she had to leave her parent's house. The same attitude is seen even today. Altekar (1938) remarks that the birth of a male child was marked with joyous celebration while the birth of a female child was not marked by any function or feast. However, in modern times due to education this particular attitude might undergo a change and people would not differentiate between the birth of a male child and a female child. Here, an attempt has been made to know what our respondents' expectations were when they were expecting for the first time.

In the present study, more than half (56.1%) of the respondents replied that they just wanted a healthy child, it did not matter whether the baby was a girl or a boy. Some (16.8%) of the respondents said that they expected a boy. The respondents gave various reasons for the preference such as: (1) sons are necessary to carry the family name forward; (2) they are necessary for material and spiritual advancement, are considered ritually and economically desirable, and support parents in old age; (3) son is needed to perform the last rites of parents and release their souls; (4) son is also needed to have a status in society; (5) girl child is a liability; a lot has to be spent on her marriage along with a huge dowry; (6) parents cannot depend economically on their daughters as per the society rules and religious norms; and (7) due to fear of in-laws and husband most of the time they prefer a son. Few (5.8%) of the respondents said they had expected girls as they feel that: (1) the girls understand and love their parents; (2) there is no difference between girls and boys as girls are as good as boys in all fields today; and (3) today, even boys do not stay with the parents.

Here, two of the respondents, one a sweeper in a college, the other a domestic servant, complained that, "*Pathopat teen muli jhalyavar navra bola, atha mulgha nahi jhala tar doosra lagna karnar*" (when we got three daughters one after the other the husband said that if we do not give birth to a son the fourth time he will go for second marriage). While few of the respondents said that they wanted girls only. Here, one respondent who is a reader in an engineering college said, "It is a myth that sons take care of parents in old age. Nowadays, daughters seem to be more caring towards to their old parents than the sons. Girls are equally successful as their male counterparts in all walks of life. I have a son but I feel he should have been a daughter. Girls are emotionally attached to their parents. "

The next question put in this context was, "Do you feel that every family should have at least one boy?" To this more than half (56.3%) of the respondents replied that it is not necessary to have a boy in every family. And some (22.4%) of the respondents replied that every family should have at least one boy. Three of the respondents said that a family should have a son, not for economic and religious reasons, but according to them for proper development of the nation and for balance of sex ratio both the sexes are equally required.

In the present study conducted among Maharashtrian women in Pune, the data reveals that more than half of the respondents did not make any sex difference between the children as they just wanted a healthy child, which is a significant positive attitudinal change. But some of the respondents still expected a boy to carry forward the family name, for material and spiritual advancement, to support parents in old age, to perform the last rites of parents and release their souls, to have a status in society. Few of them, most of the time preferred a son due to fear of in-laws and husband. They feel that girl child is a liability; a lot has to be spent on her marriage with a huge dowry, and parents cannot depend economically on their daughters as per the society rules and religious norms that show that the practice of inequality exists even now. Few of the respondents expected girls as they feel that the girls understand and love their parents, there is no difference between girls and boys as girls are as good as boys in all fields today and nowadays even boys do not stay with the parents. It is a myth that sons take care of parents in old age. The data also indicates that more than half of the respondents did not feel that every family should have a boy; that is a significant change. One interesting point to be noted is that few respondents felt that for balance in the sex ratio a family should have a son.

Opinion on family planning

It is generally seen that the women undergo family planning operation and not the men. The traditional attitudes that men should not undergo the operation, as they have to move out for earning, and it will make them impotent, has stopped many men from undergoing the family planning operation. It is seen that most of the time; it is the woman who undergoes this operation when in reality it is complicated for them to go for family planning operation. In some families, even if the woman is of weak health she gets herself operated due to frustration over an irresponsible husband or according to the wish of the husband and in-laws.

In this context, the respondents were asked whether she or her husband went for family planning operation. Some (33.5%) of the respondents said they themselves had undergone the family planning operation. The reasons given by them were: (1) Husband did not want to go for the operation. (2) Frustration over irresponsible husband. (3) Did not want another child so went for abortion and got oneself operated. (4) Does not make any difference whether he does or I do. In few (8.6%) of the respondents, it was the husband who went forth for the operation. The reason's given were: (1) Due to the respondent's weak health. (2) It is an easy operation for males. (3) Husband willingly went forth for the operation. (4) Does not make any difference whether he or me. Rest (57.9%) of the respondents were either newly married, unmarried or had not gone for family planning operation.

Here, one of the respondents who was a domestic servant said: *"Ek mulgi aani ek mulga jhala tari, navra aani sasu mala operation karayla det navte, khayala nasel tari thyana aajun ek mulga pahije hota. Me doosra mulacha veli gapchup operation karun ghetla, te samajlyavar navra aani sasuni mala khup marla aani dawakhanyat jaun doctorla pan shevya dilya"* (even after having one girl and a boy my husband and mother-in-law did not want me to go for family planning operation, even if they did not have food to eat, they wanted another son. But during the second child I got myself operated without telling them. After they came to know about it both my husband and mother-in-law beat me very badly and they went to the dispensary and badmouthed the doctor).

The above analysis points out the traditional attitudes that men should not undergo the family planning operation, as it will make them impotent and they have to go out for earning. The data shows that among the majority of the respondents, still it is the women who undergo the family planning operation. It can be said that traditional attitudes still have their hold regarding the family planning operation.

Opinion on daughter performing funeral rites

Discrimination of all kinds against women in the Indian society has been an integral part of the Indian mindset. According to Hindu tradition a son is needed to perform all kinds of religious duties, including the last funeral rites of the parents to release their souls so that they attain 'moksha' or salvation. If a family did not have a son, the cousins or a male relative performed the last rites. The daughter had no right to perform the last rites, as it was believed that the soul would not be released. In addition to this, male child carries the family name forward, protects the parental property, earns money and provides social security to the parents during their old age. Therefore, the male child is considered a valuable property. However, in recent times due to education a change in attitudes is taking place and one comes across cases where daughters are performing the last rites of parents.

In the present study, the respondents were asked to give their opinion on a daughter performing funeral rites. Majority (62.9%) of the respondents replied positively. They said that the daughters could perform the last funeral rites of their parents. Because they feel that: (1) There is nothing wrong in doing the last rites as girls and boys are equal and both have the same blood running in them so they should not be discriminated. (2) Today, girls are seen in all fields then why can't they perform the funeral rites? (3) Today, girls are no longer weaker; they can bear the scene of any of their parent's funeral. (4) If one had no son then the daughter should do the funeral rites. Some (16%) of the respondents replied in the negative. They disagreed with the idea of daughter performing funeral rites due to the following reasons such as: (1) A daughter cannot perform the last funeral rites as it is against our religion and tradition. (2) Girls are emotionally weak to see the last rites of their parents. (3) The soul will not attain 'moksha' if the daughter performs the last rites. (4) The girl is no more a member of the family after marriage.

The above data indicates that more than half of the respondents agree that a daughter should be allowed to perform the last rites of parents and that is a significant change and an emerging trend. While some of the respondents are against the idea of daughter performing funeral rites which shows that tradition and religion still play an important role regarding a daughter performing funeral rites.

Discrimination regarding food compared to brother

In our society, the male-female differentiation is seen even in allocation of food. The girl child receives poor nutrition as it is thought that she has to remain at home doing housework, while the boy has to move out to earn, he is the inheritor of family resources so he has to be strong and healthy. It has been seen that the death of girl infants is more due to malnutrition. Pant (1995) focused on the status of the girl child and pointed out that health, nutrition and education are the three vital aspects that have been adverse to the girl children and women of the Indian society. A study by Behura and Mohanty (2005) concluded that the age-old traditions and the traditional mindsets of both the women as well as men are the main reasons behind the plight of women in patriarchal societies.

In the present study, the respondents were asked whether they felt at any time they were being discriminated regarding food as compared to their brothers. Majority (69.5%) of the respondents said that they were not discriminated with regard to food with their brothers and few (5.8%) of the respondents felt that they were discriminated regarding food as compared to their brothers. They said that the brother got food first and whatever he demanded. One respondent said, "I still remember when we were small, we were three sisters and one brother, my mother gave milk daily to my brother and we got milk occasionally on birthdays and festivals. Maybe he was the youngest of all so he was pampered, even I didn't feel bad at that time but now when I recollect it I feel bad." Another respondent said, "My brother was the eldest in the house and he was a darling of my mother. He got whatever he demanded to eat, whenever he asked for something special my mother prepared it immediately for him but she never did it for both of us sisters. Now, we all are married but still my mother favours him for everything, takes his side even if he is wrong. His decision is final in everything. My mother took VRS and gave all the money for my brother's new house. She didn't give us anything." This respondent was literally crying while narrating this to the researcher.

The above data reveals that though majority of the respondents did not feel that they were discriminated regarding food as compared to their brothers, that is a noteworthy change; but few of the respondents were discriminated in this matter. Though the percentage is very small, this shows that girls are still discriminated with regard to food as compared to boys.

Custom of having meals after serving all the family members

In the traditional families, husbands and wives never ate together. The typical pattern was that the wife had to first serve the husband as he was considered 'God' and then children of the household and to eat alone in the end. It was the custom of the housewife to eat only after the members of the household, including the servants had taken their meals. It was the virtue of the 'Grihastha' to offer food to everyone and finally eat whatever remained. In joint families, the elder males, females and children were given priority. The position is, however, changing. The husband is no longer considered 'God'. He is a friend and life partner. According to Ram Ahuja (1994: 59), taking meals together is very important for 'companionship' in the family, especially for husband and wife.

In the present study regarding the question of taking meals, some (35.1%) of the respondents had their meals according to the situation. Some (33%) of the respondents had their meals with all the family members. Few of the respondents (6.3%) had the meals with their husbands. Few of the respondents (4.3%) had their meals after all the family members had eaten.

The above analysis points out that some of the respondents had their food according to the situation, with all the family members, or with their husbands. In case respondent had to go for work earlier than the others then she had her food before others. If some had health problems and food had to be taken at regular times then also they had food without waiting for others, also during pregnancy and after child birth one has to take food at regular intervals. This is a significant change compared to the earlier days when women were supposed to eat in the end after serving all the family members. But still few of the respondents had their food after all the family members had eaten. This shows the custom of eating in the end is still followed by few of the respondents in the present study.

Practice of eating leftover food

Traditionally, women had their meals after all the family members had eaten and moreover they consumed the leftover food. Fresh and hot food was first served to the elders and children in the family and whatever was left behind was for the women of the house. But now due to education, awareness and attitudinal change the leftover food is given to the servants or shared by everyone in the family.

To the question, "What do you do with the leftover food?", some (36.8%) of the respondents said that they gave the leftover food to the servants and other respondents (34.3%) replied that they all shared the leftover food. Few (7.6%) of them consumed the leftover food alone.

The data indicates that almost all the respondents do not follow the practice of eating leftover food. Some of them give the leftover food to the servants or all the family members share it and few of them had the leftover food alone. So it is clear that the practice of eating the leftover food by the women alone is certainly changing.

Attitude Towards Social Participation

In the traditional joint family, social life of women was confined to family and relatives. Very few women were allowed freedom to go out of their homes without escort. Women were not allowed to join unions, organizations or clubs. But, today, due to education, urbanization, industrialization and modernization, women are free to choose their own career, can decide with whom to interact irrespective of the group in which they are born and caste to which they belong. Moreover, co-education has given a chance for girls and boys to intermingle. A large number of them are working with males and are making friends with them. Here, an attempt has been made to see the change in attitudes of women and their families towards their social life.

To see the respondents' attitudes towards social participation, the following four indicators were selected:

1. Visit to the office friend's house.
2. Attitude of husband and family towards wife's friends and her visit to friends' house.
3. Freedom to talk with husband's friends.
4. Organizational membership.

Visit to the office friend's house

In traditional society, women were generally confined to home and their friendship was limited to relatives and neighbours. But, due to education and employment, women have increased the sphere of their social activities. The working women interact with a number of people. Everyone likes to have a free talk with friends for sharing pleasure and pains and for change and relaxation, so they visit each others' houses. In older days, a woman never went alone to a friend's house, her husband or children or some family member accompanied her.

In this context, the respondents were asked, "With whom do you visit your friend's house?" It was found that some (17%) of the respondents visited their friends' houses singly and some (20.3%) of the respondents visited with their husbands and some (14.7%) of the respondents with their family members and some (25.1%) of the respondents replied that they visited their friend's houses either singly, or with their husbands or family members.

The data reveals that nearly half of the respondents visited their friends' houses singly or with the husband and family members. It can be said that attitudes are changing and now some of the women are visiting their friends alone. This shows that women have learnt to maintain their family life as well as their individual life unlike earlier days when only men had a right to have friends.

Attitude of husband and family towards wife's friends and her visit to friends' house

The present study shows that today a working wife has her own social life, her own friend circle, with whom she interacts and even visits their houses either singly or with a family member. In some families, the husband and the in-laws may not like it.

Therefore, to find out the husband's and in-laws' feelings towards the wife's social life the respondents were asked, "How does the husband or family feel about their visits to friend's house?" Nearly half (43.7%) of the respondents replied that their husbands and in-laws approve of their visits to friends' houses and had no objections towards their social life and some (14.2%) of the respondents replied that their husbands and in-laws did not like their visits, while in case of other (19.3%) respondents the husband and in-laws were indifferent to their visits to friends' houses.

The above data reveals that more than half of the respondents' husbands and in-laws had no objection in their wife's/daughter-in-law's visits to friends' houses, which is a significant change.

Freedom to talk with husband's friends

In the Indian society, traditionally the boys and girls were trained to maintain distance from the opposite sex right from childhood. This training made it difficult for many people to change their attitude to the opposite sex when they grew up. Women were not supposed to talk to males; they were not supposed to come in front of them. But with education and employment of women there has been a change in attitudes. Men and women work together in the offices where they become accustomed to being together and interact freely in the office but a wife may not talk freely with the husband's friends at home for the fear that her husband and in-laws may not like it.

In order to know the freedom enjoyed by the women at home, the respondents were asked whether they were free to talk with their husband's friends. It was found that the majority (62.4%) of the respondents were free to talk with their husband's friends and some (10.7%) of the respondents were not free to talk with their husband's friends, as their husband's did not like it.

The above data reveals that majority of the respondents were free to talk with their husband's friends, which is an emerging trend.

Organizational membership

A striking trend in recent times is the emergence of several types of women's organizations where women are becoming active members and contributing their mite in removing the disabilities of women. Some of these organizations have been formed at the national, state and even at the local levels. In many cities, local organizations exist such as 'mahila mandals', 'bhajan mandali', NGOs. Some organizations exist even in the society or residential areas so that women can come together to have recreation and also do some social work. These organizations give women an opportunity to express their problems, promote socialization, create awareness and also help in bringing the desired change. But yet most of the women are not aware of such organizations. And even those who are aware may not find time to join these organizations as they are stuck up in household work and office work and sometimes their family may not like it, and sometimes women themselves are not interested in such organizations.

Therefore, to know the respondents' awareness and interest about such organizations they were asked whether they were members of any association or 'mandal'. Out of the total (73.1%) married respondents, few (5.3%) of the respondents were members of chit fund, a small number (5.6%) of the respondents members of NGO, a few (3%) of the respondents were members of 'bhajan mandali' and the rest (9.4%) of the respondents were members at the society/residential areas. More than half (56.3%) of the respondents were not members of any organization.

Those who were members of the above organizations were asked to specify the activities that they did in these associations or 'mandals'. Few (7.9%) of the respondents were involved in the socio-religious and cultural activities in their residential areas, while some (7.6%) of the respondents were doing social work through NGOs at residential areas, whereas some others (3.6%) organized kitty parties and picnics in the society/residential areas and the rest (2.8%) of the respondents organized visits to religious places. A negligible number (0.5%) of the respondents were involved in other activities such as helping the poor, teaching the poor children at individual level.

The above data indicates that women's participation in associations or 'mandals' is limited. Even today, women are not participating in voluntary organizations. It seems that the traditional constraints regarding women's family duties and family life are not allowing women to be active members of organizations.

So it can be concluded that the traditional attitudes towards the socialization of women are changing. In the present study, there are some emerging trends such as: (a) Majority of the women are having their own office friends and they visit friends' houses either with family member or alone. (b) The husband and in-laws do not have any objection to it. (c) Majority of the women are also free to talk with their husband's friends. On the whole, it can be said that the respondents' husbands and in-laws are progressive and they allow the respondents to have a social life of their own. And majority of the women have learnt to have their own social life along with family life. But when it comes to participation in various organizations, then the membership of the respondents is limited, as it seems that even today there is strong impact of traditional duties and they are not much aware about the nature of such organizations.

Decision-making among Unmarried Women

This sub-section on decision-making process among unmarried women concentrates on three vital aspects of their daily life. First, whether unmarried women get freedom in certain things in day-to-day life, secondly, their involvement in the family decisions and thirdly, their opinion on important decisions of their life.

Relationship between the parents and daughters in a traditional family was based more upon respect and fear. The patriarch was the one who decided everything right from the school, occupation and mate for the daughters. The daughters were not supposed to argue or talk back to the parents and elders. On the death of the patriarch, the authority passed to the next eldest male. In the traditional Indian society, the unmarried woman or the daughter was under strict supervision of her parents right from childhood to adulthood. Their behaviours, their attitudes, the role they had to perform, as a daughter were all fixed. After marriage, they were under the hold of their husbands and in old age they were at the mercy of their sons. They had no decision-making powers and no independent identity. They had no freedom in doing things as they wanted.

But, in recent times, due to education the familial restrictions on them are losing hold. But still the families function within the social, religious and community framework and are sensitive to the public remarks. The process of socialization that the children go through in the homes is important particularly during their growing years. Parents, elders in the family, even elders in the society and teachers discipline children in general and particularly girls. The socialization process is the basis of all other issues concerned with the girl child's development. Much of the aspirations and achievements of the girl child are dependent on those values and processes of socialization within the family. The present section aims at exploring the emerging role of the daughter under the changing socio-cultural environment.

Freedom in Certain Things in Day-to-Day Life

In the traditional family, the children and especially the growing girls used to be under strict supervision. In the socializing of daughters, the parental control played a vital role. In certain families, the daughters do not have freedom in matters of day-to-day life like going out with friends, going for movies, talking with boys, to move alone without an escort and so on. But, in recent times, due to education and awareness, attitudes are changing and the familial restrictions are gradually losing hold. Margaret Cormack (1961) found that the children speak in front of the adults, spend money as they choose, select their own clothes, and go out unaccompanied. When she asked her respondents how they would raise their children nearly half of them said that they would raise their children with more freedom than with what they were raised. In this connection, she also found that the children even oppose the parents if their wishes and views clash with the traditional ways of their parents.

In order to understand the amount of freedom given to daughters by their parents in day-to-day life, the following six indicators of independent decision or freedom from the parents were selected such as:

1. Freedom to go to movies with friends
2. Making friendship with boys
3. Freedom to move alone
4. Opinion about dressing
5. Restrictions regarding dresses such as jeans with short tops, low waist jeans and mini skirts by parents
6. Freedom within certain boundaries/limitations

Freedom to go to movies with friends

Going out with friends to movies was not considered good for girls as it was considered harmful to the reputation of the girl and also to the status of the family.

In the present study, almost all, i.e., 80(20.3%) respondents were given freedom to go for movies, while only 4(1%) respondents were not free to go for movies with friends.

This shows that the parents are liberal about their daughter going for movies with friends.

Making friendship with boys

It was considered undesirable for the unmarried girls to mix up with boys or to move in a social circle. Parents feared that this will not only adversely affect their reputation in society but also create problems for her marriage. But recent changes have granted more freedom to the unmarried girls.

In the present study, majority, i.e., 69(17.5%) of the respondents were free to make friendship with boys and only 15(3.8%) respondents were not allowed to make friendship with boys. One of the respondents, who was an engineering student, said, "I have more boys as friends than girls as I feel girls are narrow-minded and at times they don't help their best friends also. Girls talk about their own friends badly behind their backs. In contrast, boys are broad-minded and helping in nature. My parents know about it and they don't restrict me from making friends with boys."

This shows the changed attitude of the parents towards their daughters' friendship with boys and also the girls' relaxed attitude towards the boys.

Freedom to move alone

Girls have been prohibited to move freely alone outside their homes without an escort because of fear of social censure. Whatever major or minor decisions they made were with the consent of the parents. But recent changes have given more freedom to the girls and this change is more visible in urban areas.

In the present study, majority, i.e., 65(16.5%) of the respondents were free to move alone and 19(4.8%) were restricted to move alone by the parents.

The above data indicates that the attitudes of the parents are changing and the rigidity towards the free movement of unmarried girls is decreasing.

Opinion about dressing

According to tradition, the women were supposed to remain in 'purdah'. They were not supposed to expose themselves as it could attract the attention of men. The girl child was taught right from childhood to cover herself from head to toe, sit with her legs close, and keep her head down and so on. She did not have freedom to choose her own clothes. Education fostering liberal thoughts helped women to step out of the traditional restrictions. They took up jobs leading to change in norms as well. As they had to move out of the confines of the house for education and employment they wanted comfort and convenience in their dressing pattern.

In order to assess the changing trends in dressing pattern, the respondents were asked their opinions about dressing. It was found that, 84(21.3%) respondents felt that 'salwar kameez' is good as it suits the Indian culture, it is not exposing and can be worn by women of any age. Similarly, almost 81(20.5%) respondents for the same reason favoured 'saree'. However, three of them said that 'saree' is bad as it exposes and gives a sexy look. Almost 70(17.7%) respondents replied that 'churidhar kurta' is good as it suits Indian culture, does not expose, gives a comfortable feel and can be worn by women of any age. Around 61(15.5%) respondents felt that jeans with long tops is good as it is not exposing, gives a comfortable feel, can be worn by women of any age. Nearly 29(7.4%) respondents said that jeans with short tops is good as it is today's fashion and gives a smart look and 16(4.1%) respondents held that low waist jeans are good as it is today's fashion, is comfortable, and compels one to remain slim. Only 5(1.3%) respondents approved that mini skirt is good and looks good on teenagers. They also said that any dress can be worn but one should know how to carry oneself confidently and it depends on the individual wish.

The above analysis indicates that with regard to dressing patterns in majority of the respondents tradition still rules their opinion, as most of the respondents preferred 'salwar kameez', 'saree', 'churidhar kurta' and jeans with long tops. Few of the respondents said that jeans with short tops, low waist jeans and mini skirts are good as it is today's fashion, is comfortable, and compels one to remain slim, and gives one a smart look.

Restrictions regarding dresses such as jeans with short tops, low waist jeans and mini skirts by parents

It is seen that though few of the respondents themselves like to dress up in modern dresses such as low waist jeans, short tops, mini skirts and so on, their parents may not like them wearing such dresses. To explore, if they face any restrictions, the following question was put to them, "Do your parents restrict you from wearing any of the above dresses?" To this nearly all, i.e., 79(20%) respondents said that they were restricted from wearing mini skirts and 64(16.2%) respondents were restricted from wearing low waist jeans and 29(7.4%) respondents were prohibited from wearing jeans with short tops. Here, three of the respondents who were students said that they themselves did not like to wear such dresses. The respondents said that their parents do not allow them to wear such dresses because of our tradition and the social, religious, ethical and moral values.

The above analysis points out that mini skirt is the most restricted dress by the parents and then low waist jeans. The least restricted dress is jeans with short tops. This shows that parents still want their daughters to wear traditional dresses such as 'saree', 'salwar kurta', 'churidhar kurta', and jeans with long tops because of their social, religious and moral values.

Freedom within certain boundaries/limitations

In the traditional society, girls were not at all allowed freedom in day-to-day matters such as moving out alone, going to movies with friends, and talking with boys and so on. Many families adopted a traditional way of socializing girls, which was different from boys. However, due to avenues of socio-cultural change, there is a considerable change in the thinking of parents regarding socialization of girls.

We have seen that the respondents were given freedom in matters of going to movies with friends, making friendship with boys and moving alone. The researcher wanted to see whether this freedom was provided to the respondents within certain limitations. So, in this context, the respondents were asked, "Whether the parents have provided the respondents adequate freedom within certain boundaries/limitations?" Almost all, i.e., 80(20.3%) respondents replied 'yes', that is, they get freedom but with certain limitations. Only 4(1%) respondents replied 'no' as they were not given freedom at all, the parents always kept a check on them. Three respondents who were doing graduation said, "Our parents have given us freedom, but at the same time they keep an eye on us like who are our friends and we are supposed not to stay late in the evenings outside, or go for late night shows of movies and so on. They trust us and we will never misuse the freedom given to us. We know that freedom has certain limitations."

The above analysis shows that most of the respondents respect the parents and do not take any decisions without the parents' knowledge though the parents have given them freedom. They know that this freedom had some limitations. It is seen that parents have indeed become more liberal and progressive with regard to unmarried girls.

The present study was conducted among Maharashtrian girls in Pune and we can conclude that Maharashtrian parents' attitude towards their daughters is forward-looking and liberal, may be because Maharashtra is a social reformist state and more safe for women and the respondents themselves have shown more casual and informal attitude towards friendship with boys, moving alone and going for movies with friends. But as far as dressing pattern is concerned for majority of the respondents' tradition still rules their opinion, as most of the respondents preferred 'salwar kameez', 'saree', 'churidhar kurta' and jeans with long tops. The analysis also points out that mini skirt is the most restricted dress by the parents and then low waist jeans. This shows that parents still want their daughters to wear traditional dresses such as 'saree', 'salwar kameej', 'churidhar kurta' and jeans with long tops because of their social, religious and moral values.

Involvement in Family Decisions

Usually, the children, particularly the girls, were not consulted while taking decisions in the family. Whatever the decision the family took, girls simply had to nod their heads. It was considered bad manners to argue and talk back. But today under the changed circumstances the children are free to talk with their parents and are involved in the family decisions. M.S. Gore (1968) emphasized that only a small number of children take their own decisions, whether it is choice of schooling, occupation or spouse. However, he found that majority of the children discussed their problems with the parents and few of them left the final decision to the eldest male. Kapadia (1966), in his study of adolescent high school students, found that more than half of the respondents of his sample talked freely with their parents at meals and at other times also and this freedom is enjoyed more in the urban than the rural areas. So in recent times the process of socialization of children has changed and because of the freedom enjoyed, children today get an opportunity to accomplish their aspirations.

In order to understand the daughters' involvement in process of decision-making in family, the following four indicators of decision-making were selected such as:

1. Involvement in decision of shopping for the family
2. Involvement in shopping for the respondent's requirements
3. Involvement of the respondent in family finance
4. Taking decisions without consulting parents

Involvement in decision of shopping for the family

Traditionally, Indian women were confined to household affairs. They were not allowed to participate in outdoor activities. Even while shopping for the family, the girls were not taken into consideration. But today shopping has become a type of family outing, even for buying something for the house or for purchasing any item for any family member; all the family members get together to do the shopping whether it is clothes, furniture, appliances, grocery, crockery and so on. They enjoy the shopping experience and everybody's opinions and views are considered while shopping.

In this context, the question put to the respondents was, "Whether the respondent is involved in shopping for the family?" About 84(21.3%) respondents replied that they were involved in family shopping for almost all household items such as clothes, furniture, appliances, grocery, crockery and so on.

The above data shows that all the unmarried daughters' opinion and views are taken into account in shopping for all household items for the family.

Involvement in shopping for personal requirements

In traditional Indian society, the women lived under the authoritarian control of the patriarch, they did not play any role in family decisions and were expected to obey their parents before marriage and their husbands, in-laws after marriage. Even in simple things like shopping for their own requirements their likes and dislikes were not considered. But today the situation has changed altogether. They are no more required to look to their masters for initiative or decision.

In this context, the question put was, "Whether the respondent is considered while shopping for her requirements"? Here, all the 84(21.3%) respondents replied in positive. They said that they were involved in shopping for their own requirements and sometimes the respondents themselves did the purchasing for their own requirements.

It is clear from the above data that today the unmarried daughters take independent decisions regarding the shopping for their own requirements.

Involvement of the respondent in family finance

The family has to keep track of its finances as every family's income is fixed. Family finance means the amount a family spends on things such as food, clothing, entertainment, planning vacations, health care, savings, education, pocket money to children, transportation and household budget which means everything from phone bills, electricity bills, grocery, emergency expenses, all that is needed to maintain a house. The family has to think, plan a budget and stick to it. In planning the family budget, everyone in the family has to sit down while planning so that every member in the family knows about it so that he/she will spend accordingly.

In a traditional family, all earnings were pooled by the head of the family and he was responsible for the family budgeting. The women of the house were often ignorant of the family finance. Their job was to look after the household duties like cooking, cleaning, washing and taking care of the children. The unmarried girls were kept away from all these matters. However, a change is occurring and women are asserting their right in controlling the family finance. They feel that they should also be involved in planning and budgeting, as it is they who run the house. Even the unmarried girls feel that they should have knowledge of the family finances.

In this context, the question put was, "Whether the respondent is involved in the family finance"? Almost 58(14.7%) respondents stated that they were considered in the family finances and 26(6.6%) respondents stated that they were not considered.

The data reveals that most of the respondents were involved in the family finances and in planning the family budget, that is an emerging trend. But few of the respondents were not involved in family finances as their families felt that the daughters were young, immature and that they should concentrate on their education and career instead of taking the tension of family finances.

Taking decisions without consulting parents

In a traditional family, power and authority was based upon generation, sex and age. The oldest man in the family was the head of the family and it was he who decided on almost everything. He was not obliged to consult the children on any matter. His decision was final and nobody dared to go against him. But today children respect the elders but they do not like the coercion of views of elders on them. They even oppose if their ideologies clash with those of their parents and do not hesitate to take their own decisions. Desai (1953) found that there is a severe strain on the parent-children relationship in present-day families. He further reported that the youngsters feel that the elders try to impose their authoritarian behaviour on them and that their individualism is curbed due to the parents' strictness.

The question put to the respondents was, "Whether they take all decisions for themselves without consulting their parents"? Here, almost 82(20.8%) respondents answered in negative. They said that they never take any decision without consulting their parents and only 2(0.5%) respondents answered in positive. They said that they always take independent decisions without consulting their parents. The two respondents explained that their parents were very strict with them and so sometimes they decided on their own without the knowledge of their parents, like going to movies, outings, making friendship with boys.

The analysis indicates that almost all the respondents give respect to their parents and give credit to their opinions and never decide on anything without consulting the parents. So before taking any decision they talk with their parents and then decide.

So it can be concluded that as far as shopping for the family and for the respondents' requirements, almost all the parents like to take their daughters' views and all the respondents are given freedom regarding shopping for the family and shopping for their requirements, but when it comes to family finances few of the parents do not like the daughters' involvement. May be the parents feel that the respondents are young and not mature enough to be burdened with family finance matters. It is also seen that the respondents respect their parents and rarely think of opposing them and they do not like to take any decision without talking and consulting their parents. This shows that the respondents of the present study respect their parents and the elders also do not try to impose the traditional ways on the respondents.

Opinion on Important Decisions of Life

A clear picture of the traditional society shows that a woman's world was her home and her role was that of a dependent person. Bereft of education she lay in the darkness of ignorance. A girl was always considered as somebody's property and so the parents were unwilling to spend on the education of the girl, who would be given away in marriage. She had no decision-making powers of her own regarding her own marriage, the type of partner she would like to have, the number of children she would like to have and so on. She was so much suppressed that she did not even have her own opinions.

But recently due to education there is a greater awareness among women about their social rights and social responsibilities. With the process of change and progress there has been a considerable change in thinking outlook and values of Indian women. They are realizing that they have their own individuality and they can use their talents in a constructive and creative way to be economically independent. She has realized that as a person she has the right to take decisions on important decisions of her life.

In order to understand the respondents' decisions on the important aspects of their life, the following six indicators were selected:

1. Opinion about marriage and career
2. Opinion on continuation of job after marriage
3. Opinion on type of marriage
4. Opinion on right age for marriage
5. Opinion about important traits in the choice of husband
6. Opinion about family size

Opinion about marriage and career

Marriage and motherhood are considered the most honourable and religiously valuable achievements for a woman. Generally, it is seen that as soon as a girl completes her education the parents are in a hurry to get her married. Usually girls do something to pass their time before marriage, and one way of filling the gap is to take up a job, which is readily available to them till they get married. Traditional society never approved the employment of unmarried girls. But in recent times due to education and rising aspirations of being independent, most of them think about a career before getting married. Marriage choices are very much linked with economic and cultural conditions. L.G. Baker (1967), M. Adams (1976) and R. Braito and D. Anderson (1983) noted that in recent years, the increasing incidence of singlehood among middle-class women is due to their economic independence. According to Adams (1972), factors that make singlehood attractive in comparison to marriage are freedom from restrictions of a binding relationship, preserving personal independence, self-expression through work, freedom of movement, and preoccupation with expanding experiences. Stein (1976) maintains that singlehood can provide fulfilment with marriage no longer necessary for emotional support, an active social life or sex.

In this context, the respondents were asked, "What according to you is important – career or marriage?" The data was collected from 84 unmarried girls. Majority of the respondents 66(16.7%) said that one should be settled in career, as they will have financial independence, more status and confidence in doing things and then only one must get married. They also felt that personal growth is not possible after marriage as it puts a lot of restrictions and extra burden. Only 7(1.8%) respondents said that one should get married first as marriage gives stability, makes life disciplined, and satisfies biological, psychological and social needs. They also said that as one's age increases the chances of getting married become less and one can decide about career according to the circumstances. Only 2(2%) respondents replied that both marriage and career are important and both should happen at the right time. A negligible number 2(0.5%) of the respondents felt that only career is important as marriage is unnecessary headache and if one is settled in a career one can face any situation even if unmarried. It is interesting to note here that one respondent who was an air hostess said that only career is important and she has decided to remain unmarried, and take care of her younger sister and mother as her father deserted them for another woman. The other respondent who works with an NGO said that she has decided to work for the society but regarding marriage she said she has yet to decide on this matter. And only 1(0.3%) respondent said that only marriage is important because without marriage life will be incomplete.

It is evident from the above data that attitudes towards marriage are changing and most of the respondents consider it necessary to have a career before marriage as the respondents feel that in today's changing environment marriage does not guarantee security and happiness. Only one respondent said that only marriage is important while two respondents felt that only career is important. This shows an emerging trend to remain single. The employed women no longer regard marriage as necessary for financial support or for self-respect. There is a growing openness about the fragility of happiness in marriage. They also know that marriage is not the end of life.

Opinion on continuation of job after marriage

According to the traditional view, education was given to the girls not for taking up a job but to performe her traditional roles skillfully. For an educated girl, a job was just a stop-gap period between their education and marriage. Once a girl got married, she became the nucleus of the family, her job was to manage the house and rear the children. Men continue to think that all these jobs are to be done by women only. Therefore, they were not supposed to take employment after their marriage. Even though women worked hard for the whole day it was not valued in economic terms. But today the socio-economic changes in the country have affected the lives of women. Nowadays, it is difficult to maintain the house on only husband's earnings and this has changed the attitude of society towards the employment of married women. The women also feel that their education has to be utilized and that economic self-sufficiency improves their social status. Education has aroused aspirations for better standard of life and modern living. Kapur (1970) noted that women are taking up jobs and are continuing the jobs even after marriage not only out of economic necessity but also due to various socio-psycho-situational factors. Usha Talwar (1984) reported that one-fourth of the unmarried working women in her study expressed their desire to continue work and slightly more than one-fifth of them wished to give up employment after marriage. There were 81 unmarried working women in her study.

In order to find out the opinion about continuation of job after marriage the respondents were asked, "Whether they would like to continue working after marriage?" Almost 69(17.5%) respondents replied in a positive manner. They said that they would like to work after marriage, as job will provide them an identity, economic independence and that it will be helpful in the bright future of the children if both of them worked. The respondents also said that keeping servants could solve the housework problem. They feel that one should not waste education by sitting at home and work is important for women's empowerment. About 15(3.8%) respondents said that it depends on the situation. If the financial condition is good and if the husband does not like their working they will not work. But if the need is there and if it is the family's wish they will work.

The data indicates that the respondents are conscious of their own identity, individuality, economic independence; at the same time they are aware of the fact that money solves most of the household problems and they want to maintain it by working and earning.

Opinion on type of marriage

Traditionally, the parents arranged marriages in India. The boy or the girl could not think about marriage without the knowledge and consent of parents. The girls were not supposed to open their mouths about marriage and future mates. However, the situation has changed today. Due to higher education and increasing independence of women, they have a say in this matter. But still arranged marriages are dominant in India. Hate (1969: 66) found in her study that out of the 1,072 marriages, 889 or 83 per cent have been arranged marriages.

In the present study, the respondents were asked about the type of marriage they would prefer. Nearly half of the respondents, i.e., 40(10.1%) said they would like their parents to select the groom but their consent should be taken before finalizing the marriage. Around 18(4.6%) respondents said it is necessary to know about the life partner before marriage so they would like to go for love marriage. Here, they also said that even if it is love marriage, the parents should approve it. Nearly 24(6.09%) respondents said that they would go for arranged marriage as parents can never go wrong and they also felt that love marriages do not succeed. Only 2(0.5%) respondents wanted to remain unmarried. Here, one of the respondents was an air hostess and she said she wanted to make a career and take care of her mother and younger sister as her father had left them for another woman. The other respondent who was working for an NGO wanted to dedicate herself to social work and said that she has not decided about marriage yet.

The data indicates that arranged marriage is still predominant, as most of the respondents wanted their parents' approval in any type of marriage. A significant point to be noted is that even in love marriage or arranged marriage; the role of parents is still a dominant factor in the settlement of marriages. Though the parents take the initiative it is now an established practice to take the approval of both the boy and the girl.

Opinion on right age for marriage

The customs of marriage of a girl differ from period to period, from culture to culture and also from region to region. In ancient India, the age at marriage was fixed at a very early stage in the life of a girl. According to the *Dharmasastras* and *Grihya Sutra*, a man should give his daughter when she is still 'nagnika' (i.e., long before she reaches puberty). Child marriage was supported by many up to the nineteenth century. Shakumbari Jayal (1966) pointed out that virginity was stressed as an important reason for marriage in early scriptures written before the foreign invasion. So, the main reason for child marriage seemed to be chastity forced upon women. M.A. Indra (1940) pointed that according to Manu, a girl must wait for three years after puberty and after that she should be allowed to herself choose a groom of equal rank and caste. Vasistha observes that the girl should not permit her menstrual flow to go on for more than 36 months. This shows that both Manu and Vasistha approved post-puberty marriages. Promilla Kapur (1972) found that during the Vedic period marriages used to take place at the age of 16 or 17 years. A.K. Sur (1973) found that according to the Buddhist law the girls had the privilege of getting independent choice of husband as soon as they attained the age of 20.

But now the average age at marriage, of both boys and girls, has risen over the years. Late marriages are becoming popular. With the onset of modernization in different segments, education itself takes long time and it was also realized that marriage at a young age did not make the girls fully aware of the demands of married life and pre-puberty marriages are harmful on health grounds. The reason for increase in age of marriage is that after getting educated the girls want to settle in a career, have economic independence, a self-identity and then get married. By this time, they are mature enough and capable of looking after themselves and their interests. Also hypergamy and dowry have contributed to the increase in age of marriage. Now, the minimum legal age for marriage is fixed as 18 for girls and 21 for boys. Ross (1973), in her study, found that the respondents did not want to marry before the age of 19. Raghunanda Reddy (1986) found that almost equal number of respondents in his sample preferred the age of 25 to 30 years for marriage. Swati Shirwadkar (1998) found that some (35.69%) of her respondents preferred the age of 21 to 23 for marriage.

In the present study, the preferred age for marriage by the respondents was found to be as follows: Some 34(8.6%) of the respondents felt that 21 to 25 years is the right age to be married. And 50(12.7%) respondents preferred the age range of 25 to 30 years as appropriate marriageable age.

The above data indicates that most of the respondents prefer to get married between 25 to 30 years as they think that a girl completes her education, is somewhat settled in her career and is mature enough to take important decisions about her life at this age. The change in attitude towards age of marriage is a significant change which shows that the respondents consider the woman as having an independent identity to decide about her marriage as it is the most important event in her life.

Opinion about important traits in the choice of husband

With strides in education, employment of women and rapid industrialization and urban values, the ideas of what kind of husband a young woman would like to have, have also changed. Today, the girls want their parents to take their consent in this matter. Here an attempt has been made to know the choices of the respondents regarding the traits they would like in their life partners. Kapur (1974) found that women gave priority to a man well-placed economically. This was followed by education and good character. Pratima Kumari (1988) found that women gave importance to criteria like education, character, sense of responsibility followed by employment and sound economic background.

In the present study, it is seen that 77(19.5%) respondents gave preference to the education of the boy. After education 68(17.3%) respondents felt that the boy should be settled in some occupation. Next in preference 53(13.4%) respondents wanted emotional and mental compatibility with their life partners. About 25(6.3%)

respondents gave preference to caste, 24(6%) respondents valued financial background, and physical appearance was essential for 13(3.3%) respondents.

The above data indicates that majority of the respondents gave top-most priority to education, followed by employment, in the choice of husband. Apart from these two traits it is seen that the emotional and mental compatibility is given priority over caste, financial background and even physical appearance. It is interesting to note that in India endogamy is prevalent, but present study shows that caste is not a priority among young generation. It is shifting from caste to education and occupation. It reflects a social change from the former days when a boy from a well-reputed family, holding a respectable position in the community was sought for.

Opinion about family size

In the pre-modern societies, the family size was never restricted; children were thought to be the blessings of god. So, there were large joint families with a large number of children. Today, due to spread of education, increased level of awareness, increase in the number of nuclear families, the family is planned with each couple going for one or at the most two children. With rising aspirations and employment of women today girls want to be independent, have a career and so they cannot have more children, as it is not possible to take proper care of them. Also due to increasing prices and standard of living they think of giving all the facilities to the child for his/her all-round development. This can be possible if one has one or two kids.

Here the respondents were asked the number of children they would like to have after getting married. Close to 42(10.7%) respondents said it would be one child for them as in today's situation only one child could be maintained satisfactorily. Around 34(8.6%) respondents wanted two children. They maintained that two children were needed to learn the family values and social values such as sharing and caring. Only 8(2%) respondents said that they had not thought whether to have one or two kids or they might not like to have children at all.

The above data indicates that attitudes regarding family size are changing and most of the respondents want to restrict their family size to one or two children. And few of the respondents are not sure whether to have children or not. The respondents also said that children are a great responsibility and if one cannot do full justice to the children then it is better not to have children. This is an emerging trend.

Conclusion

Earlier, the decision-making process was clearly dominated by the male members in the family but now due to social changes there has been a gradual change in the decision-making powers with time. The present study on Maharashtrian women in Pune reveals that in case of decisions such as education of children, financial matters, shopping for major items of the house, visits or picnics, emergency expenses, settling marriages and deciding the number of children one should have, it is seen that weightage is given to the women's opinion also. She is being involved in the decision-making process in the above-mentioned matters. And, both husband and wife take decisions jointly; that is an emerging trend. While when it comes to decisions regarding kitchen matters and shopping for daily items it is still the woman who makes decisions in majority of the cases. But there has been no change in decisions regarding buying and selling of property and mate selection which are still male-dominated.

Indian society has had deep-rooted customs and practices since ancient times but, however, due to changing socio-economic conditions, the attitudes and beliefs towards the customs and practices prevalent are changing. In the present study, it is seen that majority of the respondents gave priority to career and then marriage, were ready to give freedom to the daughter to select her mate, had a negative attitude towards dowry, liked to have one or two children and the sex of the child was not given much importance, and felt that a family is complete even without a boy. But some preferred to have only girl child. Majority felt that a daughter should be allowed to perform the funeral rights; they were not discriminated in case of food against their brothers. They had their meals according to the situation and did not follow the practice of eating leftover food; these are all emerging trends. But in spite of these significant changes one thing which has not changed is that even now the number of women undergoing family planning operation is very large compared to men who are reluctant to undergo this operation.

In traditional days, the social life of women was limited to family and relatives but today due to education and awareness there is a change in attitude towards the social life of women. In the present study, it is seen that in some of the cases the women visited their friends' houses with no objection from husband and family, most of them were free to talk with their husband's friends, which is an emerging trend while it is seen that membership of organizations or associations is very limited and only few of them were members of associations or organizations.

In the Indian society, the unmarried daughter used to be under strict supervision of her parents. She had no freedom in doing things, but in recent times the familial restrictions are losing hold due to changing attitude of the parents. In the present study, majority of the unmarried respondents were free to go to movies, make friendship with boys, and were free to move alone; which is an emerging trend. But when it comes to dressing majority of them still hold on to tradition and it is seen that mini-skirt and low-waist jeans are the most restricted dresses by the parents. The analysis also shows that though the parents do not restrict the movement of the respondents, freedom is provided within certain limitations and boundaries and majority of them respect and follow the limitations set by the parents. It is also seen that most of the respondents are involved in decisions regarding shopping for the family, shopping for their own requirement, that is an emerging trend. While when it comes to decisions regarding family finances few of the respondents were not involved in the decisions as the parents thought that they were not mature enough and should concentrate on their education and career. It can also be seen that though the daughters got freedom in doing things, majority of them never took any decisions without consulting the parents.

Traditionally, an unmarried daughter did not have her own identity, she did not have her own views and opinions, she had to listen to whatever her parents decided for her but recently due to education and awareness there has been a change in the outlook and thinking among the unmarried women also. The data shows that majority of the respondents gave priority to career before getting married, wanted to continue working even after marriage, for them the right age for marriage was 25 to 30 years, they gave top-most priority to education and then occupation in the choice of husband, regarding family size most of them wanted to have one or two children and few were not sure whether to have a child or not; which can all be said to be emerging trends. While regarding type of marriage there is not much change as almost all of them wanted parents' consent in any type of marriage.

II

Role Fluidity between Husband and Wife or Male and Female

This part concentrates on role fluidity between husband and wife or between male and female. When mankind shifted to settled habitat and agricultural economy from the hunter-gatherer type of economy, it gave rise to division of labour between male and female. Due to biological reasons such as pregnancy, child-rearing, women were supposed to take care of the house and children. Due to the physical strength of man he was supposed to go out and earn for the family. Therefore, men enjoyed exclusive rights and a preferential position in the family. As the traditional division of labour in the family was such that the sole responsibility of earning was on the man and the woman was responsible for looking after the home and children. The traditional duties assigned to a woman were those of cooking, washing, dusting, cleaning, etc. Women were required to do these tasks, as they were considered physically weak; moreover they had to go through pregnancy, childbirth and breast-feeding. Due to these demands they were supposed to be easily available and not placed far from the home. Housework was tedious and endless so sharing of work by the different family members was a method to lessen the burden.

Recently, due to increase in employment of women, the traditional division of labour has been affected. When male and female both share the responsibility of earning, the housework is required to be shared by both as both have almost equal time available leading to equality of status. The inequalities in the division of labour and decision-making in the family have in recent times given rise to serious debate. Also, due to education and change in attitudes, the wives, even if not employed, want their husbands to help them in the housework. T.M. Dak (1988) wrote that this debate has given rise to two schools of thought. One is the biological school and it maintains that the inequalities between men and women are due to the genetic differences. The other is the cultural school, which maintains that culture is the main determinant of gender inequalities. Ann Oakley (1974) feels that the division of labour based on sex is not a universal phenomenon. According to her, just as there is diversity of cultures there is diversity of cultural patterns in the division of labour. She feels that gender roles are culturally determined rather than biologically determined. These inequalities lay down different set of roles for men and women and men consider it beneath their dignity to perform women's roles due to the belief that women are not capable of performing male tasks. However, in recent years it has been seen that the economic conditions account for the social subordination of women. It is believed that the economic independence of women will free them from male dominance within the family. When a woman takes up employment, sharing of housework assumes a new importance. The present section tries to analyze the nature of division of labour in the family leading to development of women. It was, therefore considered necessary to find out respondents' opinion on male or husband doing the housework, how far the family members of the respondents in our sample do sharing of housework and women's attitude towards some traditional beliefs and duties towards their husband and family.

Opinion on Male/Husband Doing Housework

As a matter of fact, to a large extent women are responsible for many a household task. But due to recent increase in employment of women and also due to change in attitudes and awareness of equality of rights and duties, the modification in the division of labour towards equality of both the sexes, becomes essential because of scarcity of time available to the working women and because of the unending drudgery of housework of a non-working woman.

Therefore, the question put to the respondents in this regard was, "What is your opinion on husband/male doing household work?" Almost all of the respondents (98%) said that husband or male should share household work. Because they felt that: (1) If a woman can manage both house and job then why not man? (2) As a life partner husband should do 50 per cent of the housework. (3) Seeing the father doing housework, the son will also learn to do it. (4) Woman has the same nature as a man and both have complementary roles to play in society and no one is superior or inferior. (5) If the woman is working, the husband should do 50 per cent of the housework. (6) If the woman is a housewife, the husband should do at least 25 per cent of the housework. Few (2%) of the respondents said that the husband should not do housework because they felt that (1) the husband doing household work is not in our culture, and (2) domestic work is a woman's work and man's job is to earn.

The above data reveals that almost all the respondents were of the opinion that the males should do household work; which is a very significant change and only few of them did not appreciate men doing housework as they felt that it is not in our custom and males doing housework is against our tradition.

Sharing of Housework by Family Members

Housework is a monotonous and endless job and sharing of housework by the different family members is the only available method of lessening the workload. Most of the women, whether employed or not employed, are busy in household chores right from morning to night without any respite, this is seen mostly in big families where the woman has to look after everyone's needs and in families with small children.

When a woman takes up employment, sharing of housework assumes a new importance. She works for eight to ten hours at her place of work and on reaching home she again devotes another five to six hours to household work and care of children which leads to problems of role strain.

In order to understand the sharing of housework by the family members, whether the woman is working or not working, the following three indicators were selected:

1. Husband's help in doing housework
2. Son's help in doing housework
3. Family members' help in doing housework when woman is sick

Husband's help in doing housework

The male members generally perform those household tasks which are known as men's tasks such as outdoor duties and earning and the females perform those tasks known as feminine tasks such cooking, cleaning, washing, rearing the children and so on. To a large extent, women are responsible for many a household task. As housekeeping is a tedious job, whether the women are employed or unemployed, the male members are expected to extend their hand in discharge of homemaking duties. The traditional division of labour is being abandoned and the emerging tendency is likely to be that of sharing of household duties.

In the present study, the respondents were asked whether their husbands helped them in the housework. Some of the respondents (13.2%) were helped in dusting, while some of the respondents (10.4%) were helped in taking care of the children and some of the respondents (16.2%) were helped in shopping for grocery and vegetables by the husband. Few of the respondents (6.1%) were helped in cooking, only 4.8 per cent of the respondents were helped in scrubbing vessels and few (9.9%) of the respondents were helped in doing the laundry work by their husband.

The data indicates that some of the respondents' husbands helped in dusting, taking care of the children, and shopping for grocery and vegetables. Few of the respondent were helped in cooking, scrubbing vessels and laundry work by their husbands.

This clearly shows that those who provide help in the house undertake those assignments which are considered less embarrassing for them such as dusting, shopping and taking care of the children. While the cooking, scrubbing and laundry work are still considered to be women's jobs. The fact is that it is the woman doing most of the housework within the four walls of the house.

Son's help in doing housework

Right from childhood, the process of socialization is different for the boys and girls. It is the girl who is made to help in the housework or assist her mother in household tasks, while the boys are not asked to do housework. They are given outside work such as getting things from the shop, supervising the outside work and so on.

In this connection, the respondents were asked whether their sons helped them in the housework as their daughters. Some (36%) of the respondents replied that their sons helped them in the housework as their daughters and some (14.7%) of the respondents said that their sons never helped them in the housework as their daughters. Rest of the respondents (21.3%) were unmarried and some of the respondents (27.9%) did not have sons or were newly married with no children. One of the respondent said, "In our house my son helps me more than my daughter and I don't feel there is anything wrong if a boy does housework. It will be helpful for him in the long run, nowadays both the spouses are working and it becomes necessary that both should share the household tasks". One more respondent who was a working woman said, "I have only one son and I have taught him everything from cooking, vacuuming, washing clothes in the washing machine to putting dishes in the dishwasher. Now, he is thirteen years old and he manages everything if I am late on some days. I have not kept a servant, instead I have brought the latest gadgets to do all the housework and my son knows how to handle everything." Another respondent said, "Today boys should know everything from cooking to washing, because for education or a job they have to go different places away from the family and they have to manage on their own. So there is nothing wrong in doing household work. When girls can earn and be independent then why can't boys do housework? There is nothing shameful about it."

The above analysis reveals that the respondents are helped by their sons in the housework, which is a significant change. It shows that the respondents themselves have socialized the sons and daughters without discrimination.

Family members' help in doing housework when woman is sick

When a woman gets married and enters into a new house and family, she is expected to do most of the housework. All the members of the family also expect some service for themselves from the new daughter-in-law. Moreover, if the woman falls sick the whole housework routine gets upset. She cannot complete the housework without any aid from other members of the family. The manner in which families manage household routine, when the woman is not well has to be explored.

In the present study, the data reveals that in some of the respondents (41.6%) it is the husband who helps, in case of some of the respondents (27.2%) it is the servant who helps, while in some (23.6%) of the respondents it is the children who help, and in some (18.5%) of the respondents it is the in-laws who help, in some (10%) of the respondents it is the relatives who help in the housework when the respondent falls sick. In few (8.1%) of the respondents it is the neighbours who help and few (3%) of the respondents manage themselves when they fall sick.

The data indicates that some of the respondents are helped by the husband, servant, children, in-laws and relatives when they fall sick and few of them are helped by neighbours and few of them manage on their own with no help when they fall sick. It is seen that housework is shouldered mostly by the husband and also by the family members when the respondent is not well; which is a noteworthy change.

Women's Attitude Towards Some Traditional Beliefs and Duties Towards the Husband and Family

The socialization for gender differentiation starts early in a girl's life. In the traditional system, the girl was conditioned in the parental family for acceptance of an unequal status. Sanjay K. Jena (1994) writes that, "the basic rules for women's behaviour as expressed in the laws of Manu insist that a woman must constantly worship her husband as a God and that women should be kept in depending by her husband because by nature they are passionate and disloyal". Her real happiness centred in her husband. Her only concern in life was to see that she properly performed all services needed by her husband. In the traditional family, the wife was dependent on her husband for herself and her children and she was grateful to him for his support. Due to the husband's economic and social roles he automatically held a superior position. Ram Ahuja (1993: 60) observed that though there is change in the husband-wife relationship, this change is not developing on western lines. The traditional outlook is still strong in our society that we cannot think of a change from patriarchal to egalitarian family. Still majority of the wives accept their subordinate position to their husbands as natural. The typical pattern for women was to serve their husbands first, give them tea as soon as they returned from work, keep their clothes ready, even polish their shoes, always obey him even when he is wrong, tolerate his tempers and so on. Even now in Hindi Indian films, dramas and TV serials of any language, women are portrayed in a traditional way fulfilling traditional duties. They are shown with big 'bindis', lots of bangles and a big 'mangalsutra' in her neck.

Now, in modern times, the roles of men and women, particularly in urban areas, are undergoing change due to the education and employment of women and also due to the democratic change in our ideas. Even though still girls are brought up on models portraying selflessness and sacrifice, mutual affection and love is beginning to appear in their relationship with their husbands. Their relationship is becoming more egalitarian in character and much more companionable due to the changing socio-cultural system and changes in attitudes and beliefs. S.C. Dube (1963) has pointed out that the traditional conceptions regarding the place and role of women are slowly changing in the contemporary Indian society. Woman, who was subordinate to man, has been put on equal footing by our Constitution. She enjoys equality in the eyes of law, however, in practice social equality is yet to be achieved.

In order to understand if there is any change in women's attitude towards some traditional beliefs and duties towards the husband and family, the following ten indicators were selected:

1. Attitude towards superiority of husband
2. Giving tea/coffee when he returns from office even when you are also tired after coming from office

3. Keeping his clothes ready when he goes for bath
4. Polishing his shoes
5. Serving him hot food
6. Not giving him leftover food
7. Keeping quiet when he scolds you even when you are not wrong
8. Always obey him even when he is wrong
9. Doing some of the traditional duties just out of love for your husband
10. Attitude towards looking after parents

Attitude towards superiority of husband

The socialization of the girls is such that right from their childhood they are taught to be submissible and passive while boys are taught to be dominant and authoritative by nature. Boys are given importance and status. Dube (1963) said, "In the traditional system a wife had to obey her authoritarian and dominating husband. She had to regard him as her master and serve him faithfully. The husband should be superior, the wife his subordinate. Hindu marriage rights also emphasize the superiority of male. No wonder, there was discrimination in the allocation of resources between the sexes – nutrition, medicare, and practically everything". But, the situation has changed. Due to the progressive legal enactments for women, there are remarkable changes in the attitude of women towards the superiority of men.

In response to the question, "Should a wife treat her husband as a superior person, as an equal or as an inferior person?", it was found that few of the respondents (8.6%) said that a wife should treat her husband as superior and majority of the respondents (73.9%) said that a wife has equal status as that of her husband and no one is superior or inferior and some of the respondents (17.5%) said that both the husband and wife are complementary, they both need each other equally and the question of superiority or inferiority does not arise here.

Majority of them no longer consider their husbands as superior but they believe in superior and inferior status of husband and wife while few feel that the husband is superior. The interesting point to be noted here is that there is an emerging thought, as some of the respondents feel, that the husband's and wife's relation is complementary.

Giving tea/coffee when husband returns from office even when wife is tired

As soon as the husband returns from the office, he expects a cup of hot tea or coffee to relax but in families where the wife also returns tired from the office cannot expect the same thing from her husband. The husband thinks that it is the wife's duty due to his superior status.

More than half (51.8%) of the respondents believed that the husband should be given tea/coffee as soon as he comes from office even if she herself is tired. They said that it is in our culture. Rest (48.2%) of the respondents said they did not believe in doing this duty of giving tea to the husband when he comes from the office. One respondent who was a government officer in the income tax department said, "*Ti aapali parampara aahe, swatha damala tari sadi khochun pahila chaha karava lagate*" (it is in our culture, even if one is tired the first thing after going from the office is to tie your sari and make tea). Most of the respondents echoed this view in the present study. Two respondents who held officer's post in the excise department said, "Every morning it is our husband who makes tea for us. Sometimes, when there are search parties we go home late. On such days the husbands manage everything at home".

The above data shows that most of the respondents still believe in the traditional duty of serving tea to the husband even if they are tired as it is in our culture. But there is an emerging trend that in some families it is the husband who serves tea for family.

Keeping husband's clothes ready when he goes for bath

In traditional Indian society, where men enjoyed a superior status, the women were supposed to be at the service of their husbands. Not only a woman had to keep the water ready for bath, but also his clothes ready when he came from bath. The respondents were asked, "Whether they believed in keeping the clothes ready when the husband goes for bath?"

To this some of the respondents (17.5%) replied that they kept their husband's clothes ready when the husband went for bath. They said that there is nothing wrong in keeping the clothes ready as the husband is the earning member of the family, he is the head of the family so he has the right to enjoy some privileges, while almost all (82.5%) of the respondents replied in the negative. They said that they did not believe in the duty of keeping the clothes ready when the husband goes for bath. One of them said, "*Mee jenva khub thakleli asthe, ulat maza navra mee angol karayle gele tar maze kapde kadun thayar tevtho*" (on the contrary, when I am too tired my husband keeps my clothes ready when I go for bath).

Its clear from the above data that majority of the respondents did not believe in the traditional duty of keeping the husband's clothes ready when he goes for bath. They feel that it is a personal work and husband should do it himself.

Polishing husband's shoes

Keeping the clothes ready, giving breakfast, packing lunch for the office are all thought to be a wife's duties. Even if she is a working woman she has to do all these things. Not only this but in some cases the woman has to polish her husband's shoes also, which is so humiliating. But some women do it happily as they think it is their duty.

The respondents were asked, "Whether they believe in the duty of polishing husband's shoes?" To this question, few (3.6%) of the respondents answered positively. They said that they believed in the duty of polishing their husband's shoes. Here, two of the housewives said, "The husband is tired working all day and if we keep everything ready for him for going to office the next day, what is the harm in it. May be working women cannot give time for such things but those who stay at home should not grumble about polishing shoes if one has to do it. There is nothing embarrassing about polishing shoes, it shows your love for the husband". Almost all (96.4%) of the respondents answered in negative, they said that they did not believe in the duty of polishing the husband's shoes. They said that it is a personal work and they should do it independently. They also said that it is degrading to polish shoes; there are many other ways to show one's love to the husband. One respondent who was a Class I officer said, "I also wear shoes but will my husband polish them even if I am in a hurry. No he will never do it, because he thinks it is below his dignity to polish the wife's shoes. Then, how do men expect that women should polish their shoes. Even in movies it is shown that the heroine keeps everything ready including shoes when hero goes for bath, such a thing should be stopped as it conveys wrong message."

The above data shows that almost all the respondents are against the traditional duty of polishing the husband's shoes as they felt that it is a personal job and should be done by the husband himself and moreover they felt polishing shoes is an embarrassing and humiliating job. This is a significant change. Few of them felt that one should not grumble on polishing the husband's shoes as it shows the wife's love for her husband.

Serving hot food to husband

Serving hot food to husband is practised in almost all in traditional as well as modern families in India. If the husband is not present while eating food, his share is kept aside before everybody sits for eating. When the husband sits for eating, the food is re-heated and then only served to him. This is a custom followed by many and it is a way of showing respect and love for the husband.

The respondents were asked, "Whether they believe in the duty of serving hot food to the husband?" To this half (51%) of the respondents said that they believe in serving hot food to their husbands. They said, as the husband is the head of the family, the father of the children, earning member of the family the husband should be given this respect and served hot food. It is our custom and tradition and has come down from ages and one should follow it. Nearly half (49%) of the respondents said that they do not believe in the duty of serving hot food to the husbands. Here, three of the respondents said that their husbands come late in the night. The husbands themselves reheat the food in the microwave and eat. One respondent said, "In our house everybody has different timings and I cannot wait to serve everybody. Even I am tired working full day in the house. So whoever feels hungry helps himself/herself. Why make such a fuss over serving food". Another respondent who was a teacher said, "After 10 p.m. I feel so sleepy but if my husband comes late I have to wake up and make hot chapattis for him, otherwise he creates a scene and fights. To keep peace in the house I do this duty forcibly even if I don't feel like serving him hot chapattis at odd times. Once I made the chapattis and kept but he fought over it".

The above data reveals that more than half of the respondents believed in the duty of serving hot food to their husbands as they felt that the husband is the head of the family, the earning member of the family, the father of the children and it is also our custom which has come down from ages and it is a way of showing respect and love for one's husband. While nearly half of the respondents did not believe in the duty of serving hot food to their husbands as they felt that if everybody in the house has different timings for eating it is not possible to serve hot food to everyone and moreover there are facilities like microwaves today and one can reheat the food on one's own, which is an emerging trend.

Not giving leftover food to husband

As the male has been given importance and superior status since ancient times it is not thought proper to give leftover food to the male or husband in the family. It was felt that as he is the earning member of the house he should not be served leftover food to guard his health and also as a token of respect. It was either given to the servants or consumed by the women of the house. In recent times, it is seen that women are becoming health conscious and they do not like to eat the leftover food, either it is shared by all or thrown or given to the servants.

The respondents were asked, "Whether they believed in not giving leftover food to the husband?" Some (25.1%) of the respondents said that they believed in the duty of not giving leftover food to the husband. They felt that after all, the husband is the father of their children, head of the family, he should be taken care of and so the husband should not be given leftover food. Three-fourths (74.9%) of the respondents said they do not believe in the duty of not giving leftover food to their husbands. They felt that today everybody keeps servants so the leftover food should be given to the servants; it will be a kind of social service. And, if one cannot afford to give it to the servants then it should be reheated and shared by all the family members. Today, we have fridge and microwaves in most of the houses so there is no harm in having the leftover food by reheating it, why should there be discrimination in having leftover food between men and women.

The above data shows that one-fourth of the respondents believed in the duty of not giving leftover food to the husband as they felt that he is the head of the family, father of the children and so he should be taken care of. While three-fourths of the respondents did not believe in the duty of serving hot food to the respondents as they felt that with modern appliances such as fridge, microwave one can store and reheat the food, otherwise it can be given to the servants, but there should be no discrimination in having leftover food between men and women, which is a significant change.

Keeping quiet when husband scolds you even when you are not wrong

As the males have always enjoyed a superior status in Indian families, they have a habit to shout and make others quiet, particularly women, to have their hold on the house. They shout at the women even when she is not wrong. May be the shouting satisfies their ego and they feel that everything and everybody in the house is under their control.

The respondents were asked, "Whether they keep quiet when the husband scolds them even when they are not wrong?" Some of the respondents (10.9%) said that they keep quiet when their husbands scold them for no reason. Here, four of the respondents said that they keep quiet when the husband is angry and they felt that the wife should not argue with him and make things complicated. Once the husband anger calms down, they make him understand his mistake. Two of the respondents said that their husbands are very dominating and whatever they decide has to be followed without uttering a single word and to keep peace in the house they have to keep mum. A big majority (89.1%) of the respondents said they do not keep quiet if their husband scolds them for no reason. Here, one of the respondents who was a lecturer said, "If my husband scolds me for no reason I make him quiet then and there only. Why should I keep quiet when I have not done anything wrong? If I am wrong then scold me otherwise I will not tolerate the scolding." She also said that by keeping quiet the woman shows that she is weak and then the husband gets the habit of shouting every now and then. So, one should control the shouting in the beginning only.

The above data indicates that almost all the respondents did not keep quiet when their husbands shouted at them for no reason. They felt that the shouting should be controlled in the beginning only, otherwise the husband gets into the habit of shouting and the woman should not tolerate the shouting for no reason. This shows that the woman today is not ready to tolerate the husband's scolding for no reason and that she is no longer weak and has her own identity. While some felt that they should keep quiet when the husband shouts till his anger subsides and then make him realize his mistake, which shows that the women have become clever and know how to handle an angry husband. Two of the respondents said that they keep quiet to keep peace in the house.

Always obey him even when he is wrong

Women always have the habit of obeying their husbands even when the husband is wrong. It is ingrained in them right from their childhood that whatever the husband says should be obeyed by them, husband is your God and it is your duty to keep him happy, not to back answer him and so on. This was so because the woman was totally dependent on her husband for everything. Today, due to increase in education, employment and awareness about one's rights and duties there has been a change in women's attitudes and beliefs.

The respondents were asked, "Whether they believe in obeying their husbands even when he is wrong?" A negligible number (3.3%) of the respondents said that they believe in obeying their husbands as it is the duty of the wife not to back answer him and moreover it leads to arguments and disturbs the peace of the house so it is better not to oppose him. Almost all (96.7%) of them replied that they would never obey him if he is wrong and they will try to correct him. But, at the same time, the respondents said that most of the time the husband forces his wrong opinions on them and they have to follow it.

The above analysis shows that almost all the respondents did not believe in obeying their husbands when he is wrong and they also felt that he should be corrected, which is a significant change but most of the time the respondents have to follow their husband's wrong opinions, which shows the forced male dominance even today. And, a negligible number of the respondents felt that in order to keep peace in the house the wife should obey the husband even if he is wrong otherwise it leads to arguments.

Doing some of the traditional duties just out of love for the husband

Marriage for a Hindu woman is a sacrament and the couples are bound to each other till death and the wife is supposed to be bound to her husband even after his death. After marriage the woman had a social duty towards the family and community and there was little idea of individual interest. The woman had to look after the needs and comforts of the husband and was supposed to be at his service all the time. But, today due to awareness of their own individuality, it is seen that most of the respondents did not believe in duties such as keeping the clothes ready for the husband, polishing shoes of the husband, not giving leftover food to the husband, keeping quiet when the husband scolds, obeying the husband even when he is wrong.

However, it was seen by the researcher in general discussions that the respondents were ready to do the above duties out of love for the husband, so to check out how many of the respondents from the present study really believed in performing the above traditional duties they were asked, "Would you do the above traditional duties out of love for your husband?" It is interesting to see that an overwhelming number (90.9%) of the respondents said that they believe in doing some of the traditional duties just out of love for their husband and the respondents also made it clear that they should not be compelled to do the duties; it should not become a routine work for them. Four of the respondents said that, "*kadhi tari karayla bara vatthe, roz cha doka dukhi va bandhan nasava*" (we feel better to do these duties sometimes, but it should not become a compulsion and everyday headache).

This clearly shows that though the respondents did not believe in doing some of the traditional duties but they were ready to do the duties just out of love for the husband sometimes and not as a daily routine, which indicates that qualities such as love, care, sacrifice and forgiveness are still there in the respondents. Moreover, they no longer consider themselves as a subordinate and they are not ready to perform the duties without rights; that is a significant change.

The above data on respondents' attitude towards some of the traditional duties and beliefs reveals that half of the respondents of our study still believe in traditional duties such as giving tea, serving hot food to the husband and they feel it is not a traditional duty, it is their duty because he is the head of the house, father to their children, the breadwinner of the family. One-fourth of the respondents still do not serve leftover food to their husbands as they think that his health is important, as he is the head of the house. It is seen that most of the respondents did not believe in duties such as keeping the husband's clothes ready, polishing husband's shoes as they felt that these are personal duties and one should learn to do it independently. Moreover, it is degrading and humiliating to do such jobs. Only few of the respondents believed in keeping quiet when the husband scolded them for no reason, as the respondents did not like to disturb the peace of the house. It shows the forced superiority of the husband. Almost all the respondents said that they never obeyed their husbands when he was wrong and they also said that they would try to correct their husband's mistake, this shows that they would not be mute spectators when the husband was wrong but they would try to make him realize his mistake; which is an emerging trend. The data also shows that almost all the respondents believed in performing the traditional duties out of love for the husband as long as it did not become a daily routine which shows that the respondents did not want to get stuck up in traditional duties.

Attitude towards looking after parents

Under the patriarchal system, once a girl got married she was no more considered a member of her parental family. There is a saying in Hindi, which shows how the girl becomes a member of another family after marriage. The saying is, "*Shaadi ke baadh hum ladki ke ghar ka paani bhi nahi peete*" (after marriage of the daughter we parents do not even drink water in her house). This was the attitude prevalent in Indian families. Even if she were an employed woman, she cannot take care of her parents even if they are in need. May be she felt like helping them, but she could not do it without her husband's and in-laws' permission. In some families, the whole salary had to be handed to the in-laws and the husband. Many a times, the parents themselves did not like to take any kind of help from the daughters. But today, attitudes are changing as girls are seen in all fields as men; traditional practices are being given up.

In this context, the respondents were put the question, "Can a woman look after her parents as she looks after her in-laws both in financial and emotional matters?" Majority (69.3%) of the respondents said that the woman can look after the parents both in financial and emotional matters even after marriage because the respondents feel that: (i) If a son can look after his parents, why not a daughter. After all the parents educate her, get her married so it is also her duty to look after them. (ii) Today, a girl is equal in all fields as a boy. (iii) The time has come when we should give up the traditional practices. One respondent, who was an engineering student, said, "Actually, if the girl is earning she should spend 60 per cent of the salary on her parents, keep 40 per cent for herself even after getting married. For the in-laws their son is there to take care." One unmarried respondent who worked as a teacher said, "The ideal situation should be such that after marriage the parents of the girl, the parents of the boy along with the newly married couple should all stay together under one roof. If the parents have more than one child they should stay with each one for a certain period irrespective of whether it is a daughter or a son." Another respondent said that if a girl is an earning member she should exactly give half of her salary to her parents after marriage also. Few (6.6%) of the respondents were not in favour of this, they said that a woman should not look after the parents after the marriage because they feel that: (i) After marriage a daughter becomes a 'paraya dhan'. (ii) Most of the times the husband and in-laws are against helping the daughter-in-law's parents. (iii) If the parents are well-settled and do not need help. (iv) If the woman is not an earning member then it creates problems between her in-laws and her parental family.

(v) Even if one wants to help the parents themselves do not like it. Some (24.1%) of the respondents said that it is fine to look after the parents but within certain limits otherwise it will lead to problems in their married life.

The above data indicates that majority of the respondents are in favour of looking after their parents because they feel the parents educate them, get them married so it is their duty to look after the parents. Girls are seen in all fields as boys, so the time has come to give up the traditional practices. This shows that there is an attitudinal change in this direction and girls are ready to take the responsibility of their parents and a time will come when daughters will not be considered a 'paraya dhan' and a liability.

Attitude Towards Property Rights of Women

Under the traditional patriarchal system, the women had no share in the property. Till 1938, the Hindu woman was not allowed a share in the joint family property. The widow who inherited the property of her husband did not enjoy the rights of a total owner. Only 'stridhan' was her property over which she had full rights. The 'Dayabag' and 'Mitakshara', the most popular systems of succession prevailing in our country, also excluded women from inheritance. So long as there was a son, grandson, or great grandson the property never went to a woman, however, close by she might have been related to the deceased. In the absence of a 'putra' the woman inherited the property but with partial assets and on her death the property devolved on the heirs of the deceased male. A number of acts have been passed for improving the status of women with regard to the inheritance of property. The Hindu Succession Act, 1956 is a landmark in the history of Hindu law as it made no distinction between male and female heirs; it also eliminated the distinction between married and unmarried daughters. But this Act did not give right to women to hold the property. Then, the Hindu Women Right to Property Act, 1973 was passed where women holding the property have full right to sell, mortgage, give away and dispose of the property as they desire. But it is seen that most of the women are not in a position to claim the property from the father or husband except for natural succession. This depends on the awareness of such legislations among the women.

To assess their attitude towards property rights of the respondents, the following two indicators were selected:

1. Whether the respondents agree to the present legislation giving equal rights to women in father's property
2. Implementation of property rights in their life

Whether the respondents agree to the present legislation giving equal rights to women in father's property

In the traditional system, a woman had no right to property. But now law has given equal rights in property to women also. However, it is seen that still some of the women do not favour the equality of rights in property as they feel that one has to spend on the girl's marriage and dowry and give her away to another family with no returns so the property should be in the son's name as he looks after the parents in their old age and carries on the family name.

So, in order to find out whether the respondents agree with the legislation of equal rights to women they were asked the question, "Do you agree on the present legislation giving equal rights to women in father's property?" Almost all (85.5%) the respondents agreed to the present legislation giving equal rights to women in father's property. They said that both sons and daughters are equal and as a legal heiress the daughter should be given her share of property. Some (13.7%) of the respondents disagreed to the present legislation giving equal rights to women in father's property. They said that a lot has to be spent, on the daughter's marriage, dowry has to be given. They also said that children fight over the property and it spoils the relation between the brother and sister and moreover she gets property from her husband's side also, so she should not ask from the brother's share. Whatever is given she should accept it happily without fighting for an equal share. A negligible number (0.8%) of the respondents did not give a definite reply. They said that it depended on the parent's wish, and only in particular circumstances like if the daughter were in need she must be given her share.

The analysis indicates that almost all the respondents are aware of the legislation giving equal rights to daughters in father's property and but some, though they were in favour of the legislation, felt that it depends on the situation and only if the daughter is in need she should be helped as a lot has to be spent on her marriage and dowry.

Implementation of property rights in the respondents' life

Law has established equality between men and women with regard to property but to what extent this law is in practice has to be seen. It is seen that most of the times even if the woman is aware of the equal property rights when it comes to implementing the right in one's own life the woman does not come forward or fight for the property rights, as she has no one to support her, sometimes she has no confidence in herself, and due to the feeling that it will spoil her relations with her brother.

So, in order to find out whether this property right was implemented in the respondents' life, they were asked, "Whether they were in possession of any property?" Some (41.9%) of the respondents were in possession of property and the rest (58.1%) of the respondents were not in possession of any property. The respondents who were in possession were further asked, from what sources had they acquired it. Some (25.1%) of the respondents had a share in their husband's property, while few (7.9%) of the respondents had self-acquired property, and few (6.3%) of the respondents had inherited it from their father, few (1.3%) of the respondents had got it in their dowry, few (1%) of the respondents got it from their in-laws and a negligible number (0.5%) of the respondents received the property as a present from close relatives.

The respondents who got the property from the father's side were asked if they got the property equally as the brothers. It was seen that not even a single respondent got it equally as their brother. When they asked the reason for the inequality they said that they are happy with whatever they got from their father and they felt that it is not right to fight for the property with one's own brother in the court as it will spoil the family's relations and name.

The above data reveals that more than half of the women are not in possession of any property. Those who had mostly had a share in the husband's property, some of them had acquired property through their own efforts and few of them had got it in the dowry, from their father and in-laws and a negligible got it as a gift from relatives. Though the respondents are aware of the legislation of equal rights in property there was not a single respondents who got it equally as the brothers and they were not ready to fight it legally, they felt that it will spoil the relation between brother and sister and they are satisfied with whatever little they got, which shows that women are of sacrificing nature when it comes to relationships and family.

Conclusion

The traditional division of labour was such that man was supposed to earn for the family and the women to take care of and look after the house and family. But now due to rising employment of women this traditional division of labour is undergoing change, the women want their husbands to help in the housework. In the present study, almost all the respondents felt that the husband or male should do the household work.

It is seen that, if the respondents are sick then they are helped in the housework by their sons and some are helped by their husbands or relatives or in-laws in the housework; that is an emerging trend. And, it is also seen that in day-to-day work the husband helps in those household activities which are less embarrassing such as dusting, shopping for grocery and vegetables and looking after children but not in cooking, scrubbing, washing that are still thought to be only a woman's work. The respondents also felt that seeing the father doing housework, the son will also learn to do the housework. According to them, woman and man both have complementary roles to play in family and society and no one is superior or inferior.

Due to the husband's economic role he held a superior position in the family and the wife had to follow some traditional beliefs and duties towards the husband and family members due to her dependent and subordinate position. But now in modern times, the roles of men and women are undergoing change due to changing socio-economic conditions. In the present study, it is seen that majority of the respondents did not believe in some of the traditional beliefs such as the superiority of the husband, in keeping his clothes ready, in the duty of not giving him leftover food, in obeying their husband when he was wrong. They were against polishing husband's shoes; they did not keep quiet when the husband scolded them for no reason. The respondents also felt that a daughter should look after her own parents in financial and emotional matters even after marriage. These can be said as significant and emerging trends. It has been also found that majority felt that the husband should be given tea or coffee as soon as he returns from office and should be served hot food. One interesting point to be noted is that though they do not believe in doing certain traditional duties they are ready to do the traditional duties sometimes out of love for the husband but not as a routine daily work. There is an emerging thought that both husband and wife need each other equally and the question of superiority or inferiority does not arise as some of the respondents feel that the husband's and wife's relation is complementary.

In Indian society, under the patriarchal system, the woman had no share in the property but today a number of acts have been passed for improving the position of women with regard to inheritance of property. Almost all the respondents in the present study were in favour of the legislation giving equal rights to women in property but it is seen that most of the respondents were not in possession of any property and not even a single respondent who inherited property had got it equally as her brothers but they were happy with whatever they got and did not wanted to fight it legally. It is clear from the present data that though the law has given equal property rights to girls and boys, the women themselves are not ready to implement the law personally due to fear of spoiling relations.

3

Educational and Economic Issues

This chapter concentrates on the educational and economic issues among women's development. The chapter is divided into two sections. The first section concentrates on the educational issues in women's development and in the second section the economic issues of employed and unemployed women are studied.

I
Educational Issues in Women's Development

The history of women's education in India is very old. Before 200 BC, the position of women was unsatisfactory. However, women were regarded as eligible for studying the Vedic literature and performing sacrifices enjoined to it. Their importance was so much that a man could not perform the Vedic sacrifices without his wife by his side. Between 200 BC to 1200 AD female education received a setback due to deterioration in religious status of women. A girl was married off soon after she attained puberty so in such circumstances female education could hardly prosper. But the women of the rich and aristocratic families received literary education, special effort was made to train these girls in domestic arts and fine arts like music, dancing, painting and house decoration. During 1200 to 1800 AD (Muslim period), the percentage of literacy among women went down very rapidly. It was believed that a girl taught to read and write might become a widow after marriage. The decline in literacy was so rapid that at the turn of nineteenth century, hardly one woman in a hundred could read. Altekar (1962) reported that by the beginning of the nineteenth century, about 99 per cent of the women population had become illiterate. The doors of education were closed for the common families. From the beginning of nineteenth century, the social reformers stressed on the importance of female education to improve their status in society. But education for women was regarded as a means to improve their status within the family and make them more capable of fulfilling their roles as mothers and wives but not to play any role in the socio-economic and political development of the country. The absence of any economic compulsion was one of the main reasons for the slow progress of women's education.

But, in the post-independent India, with the changing pattern of socio-economic and political conditions of the country, women were given status and importance of their education was realized. Education of women has expanded but is still far from satisfactory. The most significant aspect of the data on literacy which strikes us is the male-female gap. The Census Report (1991) shows that the number of male students attending school and a college is much higher than that of women. The report of the Committee on the Status of Women in India (Government of India, 1974) gave the main reasons for the slow growth of female education as follows: (1) Majority of the girls are required at home to do various domestic chores when their mothers are engaged in earning a livelihood. (2) The prevalence of child labour has been the greatest hindrance to the spread of education among the children of the poor. Exclusion from education because of participation in labour is higher among girls than boys. (3) Absence of facilities such as shortage of schools in general, absence of separate schools for girls in many places, lack of adequate transport arrangements, toilet facilities, shortage of women teachers, etc. (4) Early marriage was the greatest obstacle to the progress of girls' education in the past, it is much less now as the average age at marriage has been rising, but the problem still continues in certain communities and areas. Hansa Mehta (1981) supports the above reasons for the slow growth of women's education. Mandal (1980) reports that in Bihar the people think that if the daughters are educated they will be in trouble finding a suitable partner for the daughter and moreover they will be required to pay more dowry. This is also one of the main reasons for the slow progress of female education in most of the families.

So, in order to understand the issues involved in women's education, this section is sub-divided into:

1. Preferred levels of women's education
2. Type of education for girls
3. Staying in hostels for studies or job
4. Aim of getting education
5. Interest in professional or higher education
6. Higher education after marriage
7. Status of educated women in relation to uneducated women
8. Educated woman a better mother
9. Participation in child's school activities

Preferred Levels of Women's Education

During the Vedic period women were educated on par with the men. V.V. Prakasha Rao and V. Nandini Rao (1982) stated that during this period girls and boys were initiated into the Vedic studies by performing a rite of passage called 'upanayana ceremony'. But the post-Vedic period witnessed the deterioration of women's position. Meena Shirwadkar (1979) wrote that seclusion and 'purdah' came to be widely practised and forms of proprietary and modesty have accelerated its pace. Women's education again gained importance due to social reformers like Dr Babasaheb Ambedkar, Raja Ram Mohan Roy, Mahatma Jyotirao Phule and Savitribai Phule, etc. Later on the industrial revolution, the employment of women outside the home, to escape the dowry problem, the high cost of living and inclination towards western lifestyles have all contributed to women's education. In post-independent India, it was realized that education of women is necessary to further the goals of democracy and equality. Raj Mohini Sethi (1976) stated that when women felt that they should not be confined to homes, they started going for education in order to equip themselves to share the responsibilities of the society by taking part in all spheres of life equally with men. Majority of respondents in Pratima Kumari's (1988) study also said that a girl should be allowed to get education up to the level she or her guardian desired.

Education is an instrument which inculcates new values and liberal ideas in the society leading to development. Up to what level the girls should be allowed to get education has struck the minds of many.

In order to know as to what extent our respondents feel that women should be educated a question was put, "How much do you feel women should be educated?" Present study shows that majority (77.2%) of the respondents said that women should study and go for higher education. Some (16.5%) of the respondents felt that women should study up to graduation level. Few (5.8%) respondents wanted women to take up vocational training and a negligible number (0.5%) of respondents said that women should get educated up to SSC level.

In a group interview, a large number of respondents said, "Sky is the limit for getting educated and if the girl has aptitude and interest she should take education up to the highest level in any field in which she is interested". One respondent who was an undergraduate and a housewife said, "We have two daughters, one of them is very good in sports and wants to become a jockey so we have put her in a school where horse riding is taught right from young age, though the school is costly and we find it difficult we make sacrifices on other things. The elder daughter wants to become a neurological doctor, she is in the eighth class now but from now onwards we are saving for her". Another respondent who is a postgraduate and is a housewife said, "I have two kids, a daughter doing her SSC and a son in the seventh standard. My daughter has leadership qualities and she is the head girl in the school, very good in sports. I feel that she should become an IAS officer and we are training her in that direction". One another respondent, a teacher in a school said, "I have only one eleven-year-old daughter who is interested in becoming a pilot, we have put her in paragliding classes so that her interest develops more".

The data shows that the aspiration for education in women is now definitely higher as majority of the respondents wanted that women should take higher education. It is also seen that parents support and encourage the girls to take up education in an area in which the girls are interested; areas which are thought to be male-dominated, which is an emerging trend.

Type of Education for Girls

Education has been recognized as the most important factor connected with the developmental process of society. Women who constitute half of the population have generally been deprived of education in the past; therefore they had a more traditional and conservative outlook. In the historical periods, they were given education in order to equip them for traditional roles of wives and mothers. But there has been a lot of socio-political transformation taking place making them realize their self-importance. The notion of male superiority, the inability to take economic challenges is slowly cracking down under the force of development and modernization. There is a realization among women that to assert their rights they have to be independent economically and so they must acquire skills through education. But, the type of education females should be given is a controversial issue, like whether there should be specific areas of education for the women or they should get education in all disciplines and fields. A study conducted by Inderjeet Kaur (1983) shows that majority of the Hindu women are aspiring for every kind of education and they preferred equal education for boys and girls. Majority of the respondents in Pratima Kumari's study (1988) also said that girls should get education in all areas such as army, police, navy, forestry and so on.

In order to know the type of education the girls should take, the respondents of the present study were asked as to what type of education girls should be given? The data shows that majority (72.6%) of the respondents are of the view that girls should be given any type of education in which she is interested and is capable of. It can be any field like army, navy, air force, astronaut, police force, etc. In a group interview, sixteen respondents said that there is no limit to education, sky is the limit and she should go for as much education as possible. Some (13.2%) of the respondents said that the girls should be given formal education. Few (8.4%) respondents expressed that girls should go for professional education and others (5.8%) said that girls should go for vocational training.

Three respondents who were housewives and graduates said, "Today there is no difference in a boy and a girl. Girls are doing well and are excelling in fields which were till now exclusively for men such as navy, army, police, and administrative services and so on. So girls can go for any type of education in which they have aptitude and interest". Another respondent who is a Class I government officer felt that "if given the right facilities and opportunities girls can excel in any field as I feel girls are more sincere and hardworking in their approach towards studies. So, without any restrictions she should be encouraged in any type of education she is interested. Not only medicine, engineering, army, navy but also in courses such as fashion designing, modelling, film making, fine arts, advertising, social services, horticulture and so on. She can make a career in any off the track field also; the important thing is her interest and our encouragement".

The data reveals that majority of the respondents wanted girls to take maximum possible education according to their aptitude and liking, which is a significant aspect. The data also shows that the respondents feel that girls are serious about their studies and if given the right opportunities they can excel in any field. One more noteworthy point is that today leaving the traditional fields such as medicine, engineering, teaching, the respondents are aware that one can make a career in offbeat fields also if one has interest and the respondents are ready to support their daughters in any type of education, which is an emerging trend. It shows that women's aspirations have now started widening.

Staying in Hostels for Studies or Job

Many families adopt a traditional way of treating girls in matters such as expressing themselves freely, in moving alone outside, talking to boys, wearing mod clothes and so on. In all these areas, boys faced no restrictions at all. If a girl was interested in higher education and the college was far away from home she was not sent as it would mean keeping her in the hostel. The girl had to forego her dreams and aspirations. The biological vulnerability of girls and their marriage prospects possibly led to the girls being viewed as weak and defenceless which obviously led to such restrictions. But in recent times things are changing and one can see the number of girls staying in hostels for education or a job is increasing.

In this context, the respondents were asked whether they had stayed in the hostel for studies or a job. Here, almost all (83.8%) of the respondents answered in negative, they said that they never stayed in a hostel for studies or a job. Some (16.2%) of the respondents answered in positive, they said that they had stayed in the hostel either for studying or for a job. Few (9.1%) respondents were married before 18 years of age so the question of staying in hostels did not arise.

In the same context, the next question put was, "Would you allow your daughter to stay in a hostel for studies or a job?" More than half (54.6%) of the respondents replied in positive. They said that it will help to develop her personality, she would learn to look after herself, to handle money and it would help in her career growth. Some (24.1%) of the respondents replied in negative as they felt that today's atmosphere was not proper and sending a girl away from home was dangerous.

One postgraduate respondent, working as a research officer, said, "When I got admission for physiotherapy in Hyderabad my parents didn't allow me to go and instead I did my postgraduation here in Pune. But now my daughter who is doing engineering is staying in a hostel in Bombay as she got admission in the field in which she was interested in Bombay. My husband was not ready for it but I made him understand and supported my daughter". Another respondent who was a graduate and a housewife said, "My daughter is doing fashion designing in a government college in Pune but as the college is very far from where we stay and due to transportation problems it took two hours for her to reach her college and it was affecting her studies, so we decided to keep her in the college hostel from this year and now she gets time for some extracurricular activities also". Six respondents in a group interview said, "As times are changing we have to keep pace with the changing situations. There is a risk in keeping the girls in hostels where there are chances of them falling in bad company or bad habits, life itself is a risk but that doesn't mean that if the girl is getting a seat of her choice she should give it up. It is for her career growth so instead of not sending her to hostels we should train our girls to defend themselves, make them smart enough to face situations, instil in her good morals and values so that she will think twice before doing anything wrong".

The data indicates that though the respondents themselves were not sent to hostels, more than half of the respondents were ready to send their daughters to a hostel, that is a very significant change. The respondents felt that if a girl gets a seat of her choice and if it meant keeping her in a hostel then she should be trained in such a way that she can handle any situation as it will be for her career, moreover she will get time for other activities in which she is interested as well as she will get time to study. Some of them were not ready to send their daughters to hostels, this shows that traditional attitude and restrictions regarding girls are still there.

Aim of Getting Education

Education not only helps in individual development but also in the development of society and nation. Education helps one to move from tradition to modernity, in changing attitudes and beliefs, in promoting rationality and individualism. Education also facilitates women's entry in gainful employment. Earlier education was imparted to women to carry out their traditional roles, to lead a smooth domestic life. But now under changing socio-economic conditions, education is imparted to girls to make them independent, to develop their personality so that they can face any situation confidently and boldly besides performing the traditional roles. A statement in the Women's Committee's Report (1974) that girls should not be given any education, received a clear-cut rejection by 77.8 per cent of the respondents, but a small minority of 16.8 per cent agreed with this view. In the case of higher education, 65.5 per cent responded that a girl should not be allowed to go for higher education even if she is very intelligent. The committee asked the common people the reasons for providing education to girls. It was found that one of the main reasons for giving higher education to girls is economic. The same observation was made by Kaur (1983).

So, to explore the aim of the parents in giving education to the respondents they were asked, "What exactly was the aim of your parents in giving you education?" More than half (51%) of the respondents said that their parents provided education to them to earn and be economically independent and nearly half (49.5%) of the respondents said that they were given education to get knowledge. Some (39.8%) of the respondents felt that they were given education for personality development while some (22.3%) of the respondents thought that their parents imparted education thinking that if one women is educated then the whole family gets educated. Some (36%) of the respondents said that their parents gave them education, as education is one of the most crucial instruments of empowerment of women. Some (19%) of the respondents thought that their parents provided them education due to the thinking that education is a basic human right which leads to women's development and eventually to national development. However, few (8.9%) of the respondents replied that their parents educated them with a motive to seek good husbands and a few (10.4%) respondents said that marriage was the first priority for their parents and they were married early. Since the respondents gave multiple responses so the total does not add up to 100 per cent. Two respondents, one a matriculate and a housewife, the other a diploma holder and self-employed said, "We are educating our daughters not for doing jobs but to make them knowledgeable, to get educated husbands and so that they can make use of their education to teach their own children and if their husbands wish they can do something but only after getting married". Three respondents who were officers in a government office said, "Today there is no guarantee of the future, so the daughters should be educated to make them economically independent and also they have their own identity and status in the family if they have their own money". Two respondents who were primary educated and housewives said, "We educated our daughters and now one is a teacher and the other is a clerk. We feel proud of our daughters as they have their own money, they don't have to depend and ask their husbands for every small thing like us. Education is necessary for women's empowerment. If she is economically independent she has a status and a right in the family".

It is obvious from the above analysis that the purpose of getting the children educated falls in two categories, i.e., personal and social. It is found that majority of the parents provide education to the daughters mainly to seek employment and be independent, and they felt that economic independence gives a status to the woman in the family and moreover in today's environment it helps in securing one's future, in knowledge enhancement and personality development. Few of them gave education to their daughters as getting them married in a good family was the first priority. While some of the parents educate their daughters as education leads to empowerment of women which eventually leads to national development and also due to the thinking that if one woman gets educated, the whole family gets educated which is related to social interest. In all, the main reason for getting the girls educated is economic.

Interest in Professional or Higher Education

It is seen in case of girls that many a time due to parents' opposition, financial worries, or early marriage they are not able to pursue higher education even if they are interested. Sometimes they may get a seat of their choice away from home in another state but they are not sent as it would mean keeping the girl in a hostel. Many families do not educate the daughter up to higher level due to a son pursuing higher education or due to financial constraints. In such a case, the girl has to give up her dreams and aspirations.

In order to see whether the respondents were interested in higher education the question, "Were you interested in higher education" was put to the respondents. In the present study, it is seen that nearly half (48.7%) of the respondents were interested in higher education and the rest (51.3%) of the respondents were not interested in higher education.

Those who were interested were further asked whether they took up higher education. To this some (17.7%) of the respondents said they had taken up or are taking higher education. Some (31%) of the respondents replied that they did not take up higher education.

The respondents who were not able to take up higher education were asked why they were not able to take up higher education and what came in their way? The data shows that some (11.1%) of the respondents had financial problems so they could not continue their studies. Few (1.8%) could not get a seat of their choice and others (2.8%) faced opposition from the parents. The parents felt that the girls should get married and they got them married. A negligible number (0.8%) of the respondents had to sacrifice their studies as their brothers were studying and the rest (0.5%) rest of the respondents did not go for higher studies as their sisters were studying and the parents could not afford higher education for all. Some (14%) of the respondents could not go for higher studies due to some other reasons, which they did not specify.

Three respondents said that they were interested in studying further. Out of these, two were eleventh pass and one was under-graduate. They said that their parents were worried if they study more as it will create problems for their marriage as an educated boy will demand more dowry. One respondent working as a peon and primary educated said, "*Mee shaleth jayala radaychi pun chowthi nanthar mala nahi shikavla, pun doni bhavu maje bharavi shikle*" (I used to cry to go to school but my education was stopped after fourth class and my brothers got education till H.Sc). A respondent working as a clerk said, "Me and my brother are twins. We passed H.Sc together. I got a good percentage than him. I was getting admission for engineering as well as for BAMS. I was not put for these courses and he was put for engineering with donation as my parents felt that the son should go for such a course and I was made to do degree course. Now I feel that I have been discriminated and I feel very bad about it".

The data reveals that nearly half of them aspired for higher education and only some of the respondents were able to take up higher education and some could not go for higher education mainly due to financial worries, opposition from parents for marriage, due to discrimination between the son and daughter and some problems which were not disclosed. The data also shows that few of them did not secure a seat and a negligible number of the respondents had to give up their dreams of higher education as their sisters and brothers were pursuing higher education. It is seen that in some cases marriage of the girl is still given more importance than education and in negligible cases the respondent had to sacrifice her studies because of her brother's and sister's studies. It is also seen that even now girls are discriminated with regard to education with boys.

Higher Education after Marriage

Once a woman gets married she is stuck up in the household duties and in bringing up the children. Sometimes it is seen that the woman is herself interested or is motivated to go for higher studies. Besides it is also seen that in order to supplement the family income she gets back to education and takes up a job.

In the present study, the married respondents were asked as to when they took up higher education. It is seen from the data that few (9.6%) of the married respondents took up higher education after marriage. Nearly 6.6 per cent of the respondents opted for higher education out of their own interest, while 1.5 per cent of the respondents said that it was their husband's interest which made them go for higher education and few (1.5%) of the respondents took up further education so that they could supplement the family income.

A 44-year-old postgraduate respondent who was pursuing her doctorate said, "I got married after my postgraduation when I was working as a teacher in a school, my husband asked me to leave the job and I happily gave it up, after that I was busy in the household duties as ours was a big joint family. My mother-in-law was the decision-maker in all matters. We never had a servant in the house; everything was done by us – two daughter-in-laws. In the evenings I used to take tuitions. But in spite of being so occupied the whole day I always had a feeling that I am doing nothing and that I am wasting my education which my parents gave me. After ten years in the joint family we separated, my daughter was in the tenth standard when I decided to study further. People ask me what I am going to do studying at this age. I don't have specific plans but at least today I have mental satisfaction and would like to go into research not for a high-end career but for self-satisfaction". Another 48-year-old respondent working as a high school teacher said, "I was married when I completed my SSC after I got my first child my husband got the form and admitted me in a junior college, for seven years I studied and I did my B.Ed. Meanwhile, I got another child and now both are doing well. But if it wouldn't have been for my husband I would have never been able to do it and I will always be grateful to my mother-in-law who took up all the domestic responsibilities from me and even raised my children". Two respondents who were graduates aged 52 years and 48 years and ran a beauty parlour and a boutique said, "Our husbands' income were not much so after a few years of marriage when the children were grown up we decided to do short courses in the respective areas and start our own parlour and boutique on a partnership basis in the same rented shop by dividing it into two sections. And now we are doing very well and the family is also happy".

The data indicates that today even after many years of marriage women aspire for higher education as some of the respondents were themselves interested to go for higher education for mental satisfaction, while it is also seen that in some cases it is the husband encouraging the wife to go for higher education and even supporting her in her domestic responsibilities which is an emerging trend. And some others of them took up education to supplement the family income which shows that if a woman wants she can do anything and age is not a hindrance to her.

Status of Educated Women in Relation to Uneducated Women

As the society is developing and becoming modern greater emphasis is laid on education. Education enables one to get into gainful employment and when one is self-independent it shows in one's personality. An educated woman is confident in doing things. It increases her social status. She is aware of her rights and privileges. As an agent of socialization, the woman's education definitely affects the children.

The respondents in the present study were asked about the status of educated woman in relation to uneducated woman. The data shows that almost all (97.5%) of the respondents felt that an educated woman has a superior status in relation to an uneducated woman while a few (2.5%) said that the educated and uneducated women are of equal status.

One of the respondents who is a corporator and a postgraduate said, "In our office most of the women are not so educated either they are secondary educated or undergraduates. I am the only postgraduate so I am respected and I have a status. My advice and decisions have weightage and I feel that it is due to my education". Another respondent, a doctor by profession said, "Our's is a joint family and I am the one more educated than the others. In any matters such as education of the children of all, financial matters, and advice on certain problems in the house I am asked and told to give my opinion as the family members think that I am educated so I will give them the correct advice. Certainly an educated woman has a superior status than an uneducated woman". Another 55-year-old illiterate respondent said, "Education doesn't make one superior or inferior. Nowadays women are getting educated and are becoming arrogant with no respect for elders. I have seen educated employed women neglecting their home and children. What is the use of such education, only because she earns does it mean she is superior. I think to be superior one should have qualities such as respect for the elders, husband and total attachment to the family and all its members". Another sixty-three-year-old primary educated respondent said, "I have two daughters-in-law, one is ninth pass and the other is a postgraduate. But I think no one is superior rather I feel that both have equal status and I see to it that both of them do their household duties perfectly. I have not kept any servant for housework. I just go to the market and get things for the house, they have to do cooking, cleaning, washing, scrubbing, make beds, take care of the children, serve food to everyone and then they are supposed to have food. I have kept everyone and everything in the house under my control".

The data shows that almost all the respondents are of the opinion that an educated woman is of superior status in relation to an uneducated woman. According to the respondents, if one is educated one gets respect and has a status in the family and society, one's advice and opinions are sought in important issues. This shows that almost all the respondents are aware of the functional use of education, which is a significant aspect. While a few respondents were of the opinion that education did not make one superior, to be superior one had to be dedicated to the family, give respect to the elders and do one's household duties perfectly, which shows that some of them still have traditional attitudes towards women and their roles.

Educated Woman a Better Mother

In the past, family units were only the agents of socialization. They fulfilled many of the educational functions of the school. Today, the child is formally educated outside the home in schools and crèches. Here the socializing role of the woman as a mother is very important. Education helps in developing positive attitudes and values; hence an educated mother can put these values and attitudes in the child, can guide the children in academics and so on.

In this context, the respondents were asked whether they thought an educated mother was a better mother. Majority (75.9%) of the respondents gave a positive reply. They said that if a woman was educated she could educate the whole family and she had more capability and skill in influencing her children. And some (24.1%) of the respondents gave a negative reply. They felt that if the mother was educated it helped only in the education of the children, but for all-round development of the child a well-cultured mother was important. They also said that education was not the criteria for judging a mother.

One of the respondents said that Jijabai was not educated but she raised Shivaji in such a way that even today we remember him as a good human being. Another respondent, a doctor by profession said, "Being an educated mother has its own advantages, she can educate and guide her children but to say that education makes one a better mother is wrong as I have seen highly educated mothers not performing their duties of a mother well. So to be a good mother one should be a good human being and then she will train her own child to be a good person which is important to be successful in life". Four respondents who worked as clerks, in a group interview said, "We think that in today's changing environment if the mother is educated then it certainly helps in raising the child like helping him in his studies, in raising his aspirations, encouraging him in his chosen field, guiding him when he needs your guidance and so on".

The data reveals that majority of the respondents feel that an educated mother is a better mother as she can help the child in his studies, guide him when needed and encourage him in the field in which he is interested, that is a significant change and some of the respondents feel that a cultured mother is more important than an educated mother for the all-round development of the child and they feel that to be a good mother one should be a good human being herself so that she will instil the same values and morals in her child.

Participation in Child's School Activities

The function of a mother is not only routine housekeeping but also taking care of the school activities of the child. In the urban industrialized societies where a number of women take up employment it becomes difficult for them to concentrate on the children's education themselves. It should be borne in mind that school teachers can never replace the mother. Today, mothers themselves are taking more and more education but they also have the knowledge to prepare the child to aspire for high educational goals. Even though today's mother is busy in her own work, her educational function is to admit the children in a good school, meeting teachers, helping the children in their homework, seeing their progress and so on. The respondents in the present study were asked whether they took part in the following three activities:

1. Going for the admission of the child
2. Meeting the teacher to know about the child's progress
3. Helping the children in their homework

Going for the admission of the child

In traditional days, the woman had no say in the schooling of her children, she never went for admission of her child, it was the male head in the family who took decisions about schooling of the children. But today due to education and awareness, the woman is taking part in all activities of the child. Before the child is of school-going age, he or she is prepared well in advance to get admission to a particular school. Mostly it is the mother who trains the child and preparers him to get into one of the best schools. Both the parents go for admission of the child and fulfil all the admission formalities.

The question put to the respondents here was, "Did you go for admission of your child?" Majority (65.2%) of the respondents went for admission of their child and a few (6.9%) did not take part in the admission process of the child.

Five respondents who had just admitted their children in school said, "St. Ursula School is one of the best schools in our area; parents stand in a queue the night before to get the admission forms when the admissions start. Only a fixed number of forms are distributed and then they stop giving the forms. So we and our husbands went to stand in the queue the night before at 9 p.m. and the office was opened at 7 a.m. We got the forms and our children are in the school now. Now we don't have to worry till their SSC." Another respondent said, "For the admission of our child I wore a black and white sari, I made my husband also to wear a black trouser, and white shirt. We brought a new frock which had simple bold colours for our daughter and keeping the frock in front of her I made her recognize the colours daily before the interview day. We made this preparation as we came to know that the school authorities asked the child to recognize the colours from the parent's clothes and the child's own clothes. I didn't have a black and white sari so I borrowed it from my aunt as we don't want to take any risk. I really worked hard in preparing her for the interview as I wanted her to get into the best school and she got into the best school".

The data shows that majority of the respondents went for admission of their children and were ready to even stand for the whole night in the queue for the admission form. It was also seen that the respondents took pains to prepare the child for the interview to get admission in a reputed and good school and that is a noteworthy change.

Meet the teacher to know about the child's progress

In the traditional days, the women of the house never went to schools or to meet teachers to know about their child's progress. Their role was confined to the house and their duty was to take care of the house, elders and children. But today due to the various socio-cultural changes taking place, the stiff competition in the outside world to be successful has created awareness among the women to prepare the children in such a way so that they will be successful in life. For this it is necessary to look into the child's progress right from the beginning, to go to the school and meet the teachers to know about the child's progress.

The question put to the respondents was, "Do you go to meet the teachers to know about your child's progress?" Majority (66%) of the respondents went to meet the teachers to know about their child's progress, while a few (6.1%) did not meet the teachers to know about the child's progress. In such cases, the respondents said that their husband, brother-in-law, father-in-law, or the elder sister or brother went to meet the teachers to enquire about the child's progress.

Three of the working respondents said that they regularly made it a point to meet the teachers to know about their child's progress in spite of their tight schedule. In group interview, a total of 20 respondents said that they never missed the parent-teacher meetings. One of the respondents said, "I am just eighth pass and my children are in sixth and ninth standard, my husband is busy in his work so I regularly meet their class teachers and discuss about their progress". One domestic servant said that she went and enquired about her son's progress regularly. When she found that her son plays the whole day after school she put him in tuition classes, though she found it hard to pay the tuition fees, so that the child would be busy in his studies.

The above data indicates that majority of the respondents showed an interest in their child's progress. Even the working respondents took out time and the not-so-educated respondents went to meet the teachers regularly and also attended the parent-teacher meetings, that is a significant change. Few respondents did not go themselves but someone from the house went to enquire about the child's progress.

Help the children in their homework

In the traditional days, the woman herself was not educated and so she could not help her children in their homework and moreover she was never free from household duties due to large family and absence of modern appliances. Today, however, the situation is different, women are getting educated, family size is getting smaller and a number of appliances have come to lessen the burden of housework. Due to the time available and also because of awareness of the importance of education women now take personal interest and help the children in their studies.

The question put in this connection was, "Do you help your child in his homework?" Here also more than half (59.4%) of the respondents helped their children in their homework and some

(12.7%) of the respondents did not help their children in their homework as these respondents were less educated and found it difficult to guide their children, so some of the children went for tuitions and some studied on their own and some were guided by their elder sister or brother, if any.

Eight respondents in a group interview said that they finished of their housework by the time the children returned from school and they sat with their children and made them complete their homework. Two respondents said that during exams and before the exams they prepared the child for the exams and they also woke up early in the morning or stayed with the children awake at night when the children studied just for moral support and gave them tea, coffee or juice when they wanted. Four working respondents said that they took leave from the office during the final exams of the children to be with them for moral support and so that they could pay attention to their diet. Many of the respondents, who helped their children in their homework, said that in case of absence of the child they contacted the child's friends for the homework and made the child complete the missed notes.

The above data shows that more than half of the respondents helped their children in their homework and made it a point to take special care of the child during the exams, the working mothers took leave during the exams and in case of absence of the child also made the child complete the missed notes and homework with the help of the child's friends. Only some of the respondents did not help the child in their homework as they were less educated so the child was sent to tuitions or the child studied on his own or was helped by the elder sister or brother.

The participation of mother in her child's school activities shows that majority of the respondents took part in admission of the child, met the teachers to know about the child's progress and more than half of the respondents helped their children in their homework. It indicates that the respondents are aware of the benefits of education and so they are actively involved in the school activities of their children.

II

Economic Issues in Women's Development

This section deals with the economic issues in women's development. It is sub-divided into two sub-sections. While the first sub-section focuses on employed women, the second concentrates on unemployed women.

Economic Issues among Employed Women

Women's economic empowerment is essential for raising their status leading to their development in society. Traditionally, Indian women have had a dependency syndrome as far as employment is concerned. The ideology that a woman's proper place is the home and that of men to meet all the material needs of women and children has prohibited women to seek employment outside in traditional days. The seclusion of women from work has been an important indicator of the husband's status and success. Increase in income of the household is followed by withdrawal of women from employment. However, the restrictions against women seeking employment outside home tended to decline with increased exposure to education, mass media, etc., and economic pressures caused due to urbanization, awareness about self-dependency and so on.

The working woman is a new phenomenon in the Indian society. With increased urbanization and modernization in recent years, women of all social classes have entered the workforce. The factor which has alarming influence on women's work participation rates and productivity has been the development. Improvements in techniques of production have contributed in enhancing productivity and incomes of women. Access to extension and credit facilities has helped women to improve their knowledge and skills. In practice, however, the benefits of development given to women were far less than men. Women have suffered discrimination on account of social structure assigning them lower position than men. As a result, productivity of males increased and that of women did not. Associated with the role of technological change, industrialization requires women to work full-time away from home which is mismatched with their home-making responsibilities and thus is biased against female employment. Boserup (1976) and Youssef (1974) pointed out that the labour market discriminates against women as it is seen from their higher unemployment, their exclusion from certain occupations, lower wages from equivalent work, etc. According to Mira Seth (2001), women have adversial ratios to men in all developed and developing countries in political employment, India is lagging behind developed countries in professional and technical employment for women and behind South America, East Asia and Indonesia, Malaysia, Thailand in all types of employment. It is in this context that women's occupation is viewed as an indicator of women's economic contribution and socio-economic development. The reason for differential impact of development on women has been the control of men over productive resources and inaccessibility of women to credit facilities. Also, the extension service which is aimed to serve women is quite often male-dominated. The work participation of women is again strongly influenced by socio-biological factors. The pregnancy, lactation and caring of infants affects the duration and efficiency of work. Also, the traditional attitude towards women and their role hampers their participation in the development process.

The dual role of the women of looking after the family and contributing to the earning capacity of the family has resulted into many conflicting situations and new demands in the field of marital adjustment and family life. The career provides a new position to the women that affects their position in the family and demands adjustments in their personal and social life. So, the women's position in the work situation is an important area to be explored. The aim of this section is to bring out the prominent features of the status changeover leading to development of women and role conflict of the working women. The data was collected from 303 (76.9%) employed women. In order to understand economic issues of employed women, the following thirteen indicators were selected:

1. Kind of work
2. Nature of employment
3. Main reason for working
4. Satisfaction with work
5. Attitude of subordinates
6. Advantages or disadvantages on account of sex
7. Utilization of earnings
8. Effects on children due to working

9. Harmony between house and office
10. Conflict due to the job
11. Husband's co-operation due to the job
12. Status of economically independent woman in relation to economically dependent woman
13. Opinion on women's employment

Kind of work

Amount of participation in economically gainful activities is an index of the socio-economic background of a population or of its section. The kind of work a woman is engaged in shows how far she is developed.

The women in the present study display a high participation ratio in economic activities. The working women were employed in a wide range of occupations, ranging from professional to unskilled. Women engaged in teaching and clerical jobs were highest, 79(20.1%), next in order were women who were self-employed like taking tuitions, running a beauty parlour, tailoring, etc., and doing small businesses such as household business like selling sarees, dress materials, masalas, pickles, cosmetics and so on, there were 55(14%) such women. Women engaged in professional occupations such as doctors, engineers, principals, lawyers and lecturers were 51(13%). Women who helped their husbands or family in their business such as Xerox shop, electrical goods shop, general stores, STD and PCO booths, looking after the office work of the husband accounted for 51(12.9%). Women who worked as government officers, NGO officers, and corporators were 47(11.9%). And women who worked as domestic servants and peons were 20(5.1%).

The data indicates that number of respondents engaged in teaching and clerical jobs is the highest, lowest being that of domestic servants and peons. It is seen that women still prefer teaching and clerical jobs. There is need to encourage women to go for professional and administrative jobs.

Nature of employment

When a woman takes up employment she feels that it should be permanent as it gives her security and a sense of well-being. If it is temporary then she is in a fix whether she will get a job immediately, what post she will be getting, will it be suitable to her, what will be her salary and so on which may affect her working pattern. So, the nature of employment is important while studying the employed women.

In the present study, the data shows that as many as 52(13.2%) respondents were in temporary jobs and 251(63.7%) of them were holding permanent jobs. The respondents who were self-employed, those who were helping in the family business were included in permanent jobs.

Main reason for working

Why do women work or enter employment differs from person to person. The socio-cultural changes have created a situation in which women have to seek employment but at the same time there are several other factors which lead an individual to work or not to work. The Ministry of Labour, Government of India (1964) pointed out four factors which push women to take up employment: (a) inadequate income of the principal earner which forces the women to take up work to supplement the income; (b) death of the bread-winner; (c) mishaps, such as incapacity of the bread-winner; and (d) a woman's desire for economic independence or to secure a higher standard of living or the desire of the women to give expression to their own talents and skills. Klien's study (1965) showed that 73 per cent women in her sample worked for money. Ranade's and Ramchandra's (1964) studies in Delhi and Bombay also showed that a large number of women worked for economic reasons.

In this context, the question put to the respondents was, "What is the main reason for your working?" The analysis shows that majority (69%) of the respondents worked to be economically independent. Majority (64.5%) of the respondents had taken up employment due to economic pressures to supplement the family income. Half (50%) of the respondents said that they were deliberately working to make use of their education while few (7.1%) of them worked to help their parents and others (3%) worked as it was the wish of their husband/in-laws/parents. Few (3%) respondents felt boredom with the continuous routine of household work and to escape from the boredom and utilize the time meaningfully they had taken up a job. The responses do not total to 100 per cent because the respondents gave multiple responses to this question.

In a group interview, eight respondents said that they belonged to the middle-class and as everything was getting costly nowadays, it was necessary to have two incomes in the house to meet the needs. We can give our children all the facilities and have a better standard of living. Three respondents said, "We are financially well off, our husbands earn well, but even then we like to work, as economic independence gives you a certain status, mental satisfaction and confidence in doing things. Moreover, education and talent should not be wasted". Two of the respondents said, "We are from a wealthy family and our income is not so important in our homes, so to utilize our time meaningfully and to get away from boredom we are working for an NGO which works for orphans. It is like part-time voluntary jobs where you get a small amount as honorarium and we are happy about it". Another respondent who was self-employed and takes tuitions at home and was married said, "My husband is well settled in business, but I take tuitions to help my parents to meet their medical expenses as they get a small amount as pension which is not enough for them. My husband knows it, he tells me that he will give for their medicines but I don't like it. I feel if the time comes he will say and show so I don't want his favour. They are my parents, they have educated me, got me married, so it is my duty to do for them". All of them added one more point that nowadays employment/jobs have become mandatory for women and for her family. Even in marriage grooms prefer/demand for working brides.

The above data shows that majority of the working women were in employment on account of economic pressures and majority of them took to work because of personality trait, to be economically independent, to have a status and to make use of education. It was also observed that some respondents worked to help their parents with their husband's knowledge, they did not like to take help from the husbands as the respondents felt that it was their duty to help their parents or due to the wish of their parents/in-laws/husband or to get away from the boredom of housework and utilize their time meaningfully. An interesting point to be noted here is that a large section of the respondents were in a job to be self-reliant even though when they were financially well off and working women is the demand of the society, that is an emerging trend.

Satisfaction with work

Though gainful employment makes a woman independent and self-reliant, there are some tasks and occupations which are not satisfying and hence the workers may not be satisfied with their work. A woman may take up a job which is not suitable to her qualification out of necessity; she might be getting tired due to overwork, or may not be satisfied due to mental harassment at her workplace and so on.

So, in order to gauge whether the working respondents in our study were satisfied with the nature of their work, a question was asked, "Are you satisfied with your work?" It is seen that majority 268(68%) of the respondents were satisfied with their work and few 35(8.9%) of the respondents were not satisfied with their work.

The respondents who were not satisfied were further asked the reasons for their dissatisfaction. It was seen that 10(2.5%) respondents were not satisfied with the jobs as the job they were doing was not suitable to their education.

Two respondents who were officers in a government office said that they were satisfied with their jobs as the seniors, under whom they worked, were helpful, co-operative and understanding. Another respondent, a lecturer in a college and had a small kid of three, said that her head and colleagues are very understanding and helpful, whenever her child was not well she was given leave or given permission to go early. Here, two respondents, one of whom was a postgraduate, and teaching in a primary school and the other a commerce graduate, who kept the accounts of a garment shop. Both of them got very less salary but as it was necessary for them and due to their financial conditions they were doing the jobs. And 5(1.3%) respondents were tired due to their work as they were always given more work by their seniors. While 6(1.5%) of them were dissatisfied due to mental harassment at the workplace and 14(3.6%) respondents gave reasons such as non-appreciation of their work, extreme tiredness due to housework and office work, night shifts, temporary jobs and so on. But almost all said that financial independence was most important here, working place and condition, satisfaction were secondary.

The above data shows that majority of the respondents were satisfied with their work as their seniors were understanding, helpful and co-operative, that is an important change. While few of the respondents were not satisfied with their work as their jobs were not suitable to their qualifications, due to more work given by the seniors, mental harassment at the workplace, non-appreciation of work, tiredness due to dual duties of house and office, night shifts and temporary jobs. This shows that women are still not satisfied with the work conditions. But they are giving importance to financial independence. Working place, condition, and satisfaction are secondary to them.

Attitude of subordinates

Traditionally, a woman's place was only in the home. These attitudes are, however, changing because of economic reasons and change in social values. Today, women are working and contributing to the family welfare and national development. Many women are seen in executive and officers' posts and some men who are subordinates to them cannot digest the fact that they have to work under a woman boss. So, they resent it and try to create problems for the woman boss.

In order to probe, the women from our study who were heads in their offices were asked, "If you are the head in the office what is the attitude of your subordinates?" This question was applicable to 58(14.6%) of the respondents as out of the 303 working women 38 of them were in the head's position. The analysis shows that few 24(6.1%) respondents said that their subordinates obeyed them, 14(3.5%) respondents replied that their subordinates resented the fact that they had to take orders from a female boss. While 20(5%) respondents felt that their subordinates were indifferent to their sex and that the subordinates had no problem working under a woman boss.

Here, three respondents, who were government officers, said that their subordinates always tried to create problems for them, find out mistakes in their work and talked badly behind their backs. But they said that now everything was under control and the respondents also felt that if one was sincere and hardworking nobody could do anything. At the same time, they felt that women had to work harder than men to prove themselves in the male-dominated fields.

A respondent who held the post of an income tax commissioner said, "When I was newly elected for the mayor's post my subordinates were not happy as they will have to work under a woman. One of my colleagues went on a long vacation, he even tried to get himself transferred to another place but he could not so he joined duty and gradually when he started getting acquainted with me and my work he started respecting me and now he is the most trusted and honest person in my office. I think women have a knack of getting into details, know how to handle people and situations and it is this quality in them that is making them lead some of the top companies today".

The data indicates that a few respondents were obeyed by their subordinates, while others were resented by their subordinates as they did not like to work under a female head in the beginning but due to the respondent's way of handling the situations at work everything was brought under control which shows that women can be good leaders and managers. Some of the respondents reported that their subordinates were indifferent to their being a woman boss which is a significant change and shows that men have started accepting women's superior position at the workplace.

Advantages or disadvantages on account of sex

Traditionally, woman's role was confined to the household work but due to the critical economic needs, the education of women and the changing perception of work values have enabled the women to seek employment. This extension of the role of women has resulted in conflicting situations, as the society and men at large were not used to seeing women working, earning and being independent. Although today women are entering salaried occupations in large numbers, there are instances of gender discrimination at the workplace.

Though there is a sea change in attitudes of looking towards a working woman, in order to see if the respondents of the present study experienced any discrimination due to their sex, they were asked, "Do you get advantages or disadvantages in the office on account of your sex?" The question was applicable to 239(78.8%) respondents as the rest 64(21.1%) respondents were not working in offices, they were self-employed or had small household businesses. It was seen that 189(62.4%) respondents did not suffer any disadvantages on account of their sex. They said that their office colleagues were always understanding, helpful and supportive and they never faced any problems. While 50(16.5%) respondents suffered disadvantages due to their sex at the workplace.

A respondent who was a corporator said, "When I was a mayor during my tenure, whenever I took some decisions, I was never supported by my male colleagues; they tried to mentally harass me, so I had to work against the tide to prove myself. But once when the male colleagues knew that I cannot be pulled down they started respecting and supporting me". One respondent who is a clerk said, "My senior always made advances to me and once he increased only my salary in the office without any reason, I didn't accept the increment, may be he got the message and he started troubling me like giving me more work, no leave even when required urgently, at last I left the job and looked for another job". Three respondents who were government officers said, "Gender discrimination is there in every field but one should know how to tackle it. If it is not so serious then one should avoid it and go ahead with one's work but if it becomes serious then the opposite person who is harassing or discriminating should be given the right answer in the right manner then he will never dare or even try to trouble you. So it is up to us how we take it".

The above data reveals that majority of the respondents did not suffer any disadvantages due to their sex; they felt that their colleagues were helpful and supportive, that is a significant change. And some of the respondents suffered disadvantages due to their being a woman like mental harassment, no support from the male colleagues, getting more work and no leave when required. But an interesting point to be noted is that the respondents have been bold in tackling gender discrimination situations at the workplace, which shows that the women are no longer weak and are ready to fight against discrimination on account of sex, if the situation demands.

Utilization of earnings

In the the traditional family, the male members have always dominated, they had the right over earnings. Any income or property of the women was also under the control of menfolk. Even today, in some families, the income of the working women is controlled by their husband and other family members.

Economic empowerment also requires control over the use of one's earnings. The National Family Health Survey-III (2007) made some important findings such as only 24 per cent of the women who earned decided on how to spend their earnings while 57 per cent said that the husband had a major say in this matter. For 15 per cent, the husband single-handedly made the decision regarding her earnings. Even among the oldest age group, the most highly educated category and women belonging to the wealthiest section, only 28–31 per cent of women said they decided themselves on how their earnings were to be spent. The survey was carried in states where three out of four employed women earned in cash such as Kerala (91%), Tamil Nadu (90%), Goa (83%), Assam (85%), and West Bengal (83%).

In the present study, to see whether the respondents had control over their earnings they were asked, "How do you utilize your earnings?" The respondents gave multiple responses so the responses do not total to 100 per cent. It is seen that 240(60.9%) respondents contributed their salary to the family. More than half, i.e., 216(54.8%) respondents saved some part of the salary for future plans, 37(12.2%) respondents utilized some part of the salary to help their parents. Almost 34(11.22%) handed over their entire salary to their husbands/in-laws. While 5(1.6%) respondents spent their earnings as they wished.

Three married respondents gave some of their earnings to their parents as their parents were not so well-off financially and one more married respondent helped her parents for their monthly medicines. These respondents helped their parents and their husbands had no objection to it. Here, nine respondents said that although they were earning they did not have right on single paisa of their earnings. They had to ask their husbands and in-laws even for their necessities like transportation, shopping for their needs, etc. Here three of the respondents were unmarried and were from wealthy families, their parents never asked them about their salary. These three respondents said that they are also saving some part of the salary to start their own businesses. Two respondents were married and their husbands were doing very well in their respective businesses so they spent their earnings on themselves and saved some part and their husbands never asked about their salary.

The data shows that majority of the respondents contributed their salary to the family, some of the respondents saved some part of the salary for future plans which shows that the women are becoming clever. Some of the respondents gave some part of the salary to their parents with the knowledge of their husbands to help the parents financially or for their medical expenses, which is an emerging trend, few of them spent their earnings as they wished as their families were doing well which shows that the working women are asserting their own right in controlling their own earnings. But at the same time, it is seen that some of the respondents still have to hand over their earnings to their husbands and in-laws which shows that male dominance still prevails in the society and women have no say on their own earnings.

Effects on children due to working

The question generally asked while considering the advantages of women's employment is the effect of employment of women on the children. Rearing children is a difficult job. A mother has greater responsibility than the father in the all-round development of the child. It is generally felt that women with dual duties are not able to do justice to the children like their physical care, the psychological support that they need and so such children have behavioural problems. But there is hardly any adequate empirical study in this area. There are some studies which show relationship between mother's employment and one or the other type of maladjustment in children, e.g., H.B. Hand's (1957) study showed that maternal employment has been associated with higher child delinquency and F. Ivan Nye (1958) reported withdrawal behaviour in children. But Siegel's and Stolz's study (1959) on child development reports no relation at all between maternal employment and children's behaviour. Sylvia Hewlett's research (2007) shows that 80 per cent of extreme job holders are men where they work more than 60 hours per week and there are very few women holding extreme jobs. She further found out that 30–40 per cent of women extreme job holders felt that their kids were underperforming at school, eating a lot of junk food and watching too much television, and so women are opting out of these jobs. Hence, there are differing viewpoints.

So, to identify the effects of employment of women on their children, the respondents were put the question, "Do you think that your working outside affects the bringing up of your children in any way?" Around 143(36.3%) respondents said 'no' to this question. They gave the following reasons for their reply such as: (1) One should know how to balance both the housework and office work effectively. (2) They felt that children become independent, smart, bold, understanding and of adjustable nature right from childhood, they realize that their mother also has work and status. Some of the respondents who said no to this question were self-employed doing some household business and worked from home. This may be because they did not go far away from the four walls of their homes to work so that they might be able to supervise their children, hence they reported no effect on them. While 76(19.3%) respondents said 'yes' to this question. They said that their working outside affected the children. They gave the following reasons for their reply such as: (1) They felt that they could not give enough time to their children's studies; particularly during the exams they felt guilty about it. (2) They felt that the children become stubborn and arrogant. (3) When the child is sick or when the children need the mother and they cannot stay behind they feel bad and guilty.

Here, one of the respondent said, "When I joined the office after three months' leave after my delivery, when the feeding time came I used to feel very bad, I felt a strong urge to be with the child, many a times I locked myself in the office bathroom and cried badly. But over a period of time one gets used to it and now my children are 19 years and 15 years old, but I still feel that I was not with them when they needed me the most." Three more respondents said, "Being a working woman is a constant struggle, especially when it comes to kids. Even if you try and balance your work and family, there is still an emotional pull." Two respondents who were gazzetted officers in the income tax department said, "At times the woman is torn between her professional aspirations and her familial roles. We still feel that we have not given 100 per cent attention to our children. We feel terribly guilty when we have to go out for night search parties and these search parties are mostly in the month of March or April when the children have their final exams". One respondent who was a professor in a college said, "As I'm in information technology I have to keep myself updated. Sometimes right from the morning till late evenings I have to be in the college and this is affecting my five-year-old son. He is having a behaviour problem and if it continues I'm thinking of leaving the job and start consultancy so that I can work from home. For all-round development of the child the mother should be with the child all the time at least during the first few years". Many of them admit experiencing an inner conflict for not doing enough for the family and children. Two respondents said, "We work as clerks in an office, when the children were kids our mothers took care of them. But right from their first standard we taught them to be independent. The keys remain with the neighbours, they open the house, freshen up and went to their hobby classes and after coming from the classes they sit and study by the time we are back from the office. The children know that their mother also has work and so they have become understanding and adjustable". Another respondent working in a bank said, "I have a maid servant who comes when the children are back from school and she gives them whatever they want to eat and sits with them till I come back from the office". One respondent working as an officer with an NGO said, "I do feel guilty when my daughters fall ill and I cannot take more than a day or two off. I feel terrible when sometimes I do not have time for them, but I feel there is no way out as a woman has to have something that is all her own – it's her identity. Moreover, nowadays, expectations are increasing from a woman. She has to be perfect in her office work, in her familial duties, in her social life and so on. Women today are fighting with themselves to become good mothers and to become good employers, good in her social life. So, they are overburdening themselves. The family should also realize that after all a woman is also a human being, she also has her own ambitions and she is not a superwoman. So I think there should be a well-placed support system for today's kids".

The above data clearly shows that some of the respondents believed that their working outside did not affect their children, but it was seen that most of the respondents from this category were working from home or had a job where they could be at home when their children returned from school and so they were able to give time to their children. Even those who were holding eight-hour jobs had their own ways of tackling this problem like by keeping servant or telling the neighbours to keep a watch or engaging the children in some activities till they returned from the office. It was seen that though they felt bad when they could not stay behind when the children needed them, they felt that in spite of all this a woman has to have her own identity and so she should not let the guilt grow to a point where it affects her personal and professional life. They felt that this problem can be solved by having a well-placed support system. While some of the respondents felt that their working outside affected their children, they felt guilty when they could not stay behind when the child was sick, during their exams when they needed their mother the most. This shows that women are always guilt-ridden and torn between professional aspirations and family life. Women tend to draw a straight line between anything that is going wrong in their child's life and their own, work schedule, so they blame themselves but at the same time they feel that even they should have their own identity which is an emerging trend. It may be because women tend to see themselves as keepers of relationships. This shows that a job is much more than cash benefits to a working woman, it is closely integrated with her whole life. In addition to this they also feel that since nowadays society's expectations from woman are increasing, she has to be perfect in her office work, in her familial duties, in her social life and so on. Therefore, women today are fighting with themselves not only to become good mothers and good employees, but also good in their social lives. So they are overburdening themselves.

Harmony between house and office

Traditionally, a woman's place was in the house and her duty was to look after the household duties and children. But recently owing to the various socio-economic reasons, women have started taking up jobs but it is seen that they are not able to get out of the prescribed ideal type of feminine roles. Now, they have to manage both the worlds – their home sphere and their occupational sphere. Due to the dual roles sometimes the working women are liable to face a crisis of adjustment. Often they have to face conflicting situations due to the changed role of working outside the home.

In order to understand whether the respondents had been able to bring harmony between the house and office, the following question was put to them, "How far have you succeeded in bringing harmony between office and house?" More than half, i.e., 228(57.9%) respondents said that they had been able to bring harmony between their house and office. Most of the respondents from this category were self-employed – helping in the family business, teachers, peons who had fixed timings or flexible timings so they were able to bring harmony between their house and job. Also the unmarried working respondents echoed this view, as they did not have to bother about household duties. Close to 75(19%) respondents said that they had not been able to bring harmony between the house and office and they were in conflict. In this category, the respondents were mostly in professional jobs or were government officers who hold high-end jobs with lot of stress and strains.

One respondent who was a professor in a college said, "As my field is information technology I have to update myself with the latest technologies. Sometimes I have to wait till 8 p.m. in the college. Sometimes I am so tired that I cannot give time to my five-year-old daughter. My husband is telling me to leave the job and I am in a fix". Another respondent working as an officer said, "Sometimes the workload is so much and it gets late to reach home, my husband and in-laws think that I purposely stay late in the office and they keep taunting me." Another respondent who was a reputed doctor said, "My husband is also a doctor but I earn more than him and this hurts his ego and without any reason he picks fights with me. I try my best not to hurt his ego but it is of no use". Three respondents said that they were self-employed and so they worked according to their convenience and so it did not affect their children and house. Two respondents working as teachers said,

"Our school timings are such that we return from the school when the children are back from school so we don't have problem in managing both the duties". Six respondents, in a group interview, said that their in-laws place is nearby and they take care of their children so they do not face any problems. One respondent working as a Class II officer said, "Due to my husband's full support I have been able to do this job. Till my both kids reached the age of ten, my husband took the night shifts so that he can be at home from morning till evening with the kids. I am really grateful to him for his support". One more respondent working as an accounts officer said, "During year end I had to stay late in the office due to workload, my husband cooked, fed the children and used to put them to sleep many a times by the time I reached home. It is because of him that I have been successful in my job".

The data shows that more than half of the respondents succeeded in bringing harmony between the house and office as they had fixed and flexible timings and most of them were either self-employed or worked from home so they could adjust their timings according to the needs of the family and children. It was also seen that some of the respondents who were holding high-end jobs had their parents or in-laws staying nearby who helped them. Also due to the husband's support they were able to bring harmony between their jobs and household duties. While some of the respondents were in a conflict situation as they could not bring harmony between the house and their job as most of them were in professions in which they had to stay late in the office, the type of work was such that it involved a lot of stress and so the respondents themselves and their families felt that the respondents were not giving enough time to the family and children. It was seen that the respondents suffered from a sense of guilt as they found it difficult to carry out both the responsibilities especially when they had young children. It created a lot of confusion and conflict in their roles. But, at the same time, she said that household work problem can be solved by support system. Whether there is harmony or conflict between the house and the office work, job is most valuable for women as it has given them their own identity, their own world and financial security. And employment of women directly leads to women's social development through economic development. This is an emerging trend.

Conflict due to the job

We have seen in the previous indicator that 75(19%) respondents were in a conflict as they were not able to bring harmony between their home and job due to difficulty in carrying out dual duties and due to the attitude of their husband and in-laws.

These 75 respondents were further asked the question, "In the event of conflict what according to your will be primary (1) work in the house, (2) work in the office, or (3) both?" Almost 59(14.9%) respondents said that they would like to do both the things – work in the house as well as work in the office. Only 9(2.3%) respondents said that if there were a serious conflict in the house, and if the children were getting neglected or having some problems due to their job, they would happily give up the job and would give priority to the house and family. But they were firm on their opinion about priority to job. Just 7(1.8%) respondents said that in the event of a conflict they would give preference to their office work over house, as a woman also had her own ambitions.

Here, nine respondents said, "Our children are grown up now, when they were small there was always an inner conflict that we are not doing enough for them. But over a period of time one gets used to all these things such as conflict, no understanding by the family members, attitude of in-laws, workload and so on. It is the woman who has to make the adjustments most of the time and the time just goes on. So, one has to overlook such things and move on". One respondent who was a professor said that as her five-year-old daughter was showing some behaviour problems, she was thinking of leaving the job and work from home. Two respondents working as clerks in a private firm said, "Whatever one does is for the family and children and if the children and the family are not happy or are having problems due to your job then that job is of no use. It is not necessary that one should do a full-time job, one can do something from the home also". Another respondent who is a junior clerk in a government office said, "My husband works in Dubai and I stay alone with my two kids one seven-year-old and other four-year-old. During school days the kids have a routine and by the time they are back from school and tuitions I reach home. But the problem is during vacations when they are alone at home for the full day; half of my mind is at home. My elder son cries and is telling me to give up the job. I feel very bad and sometimes I am thinking of leaving the job".

The above data shows that majority of the respondents would like to do both housework and office work in the event of a conflict which shows that women are not ready to compromise on both the fronts, they are ready to work hard, make adjustments but not leave their jobs. Few respondents were ready to leave their jobs in case of a serious conflict in the house due to their jobs. They felt that if the family is not happy then it is better to leave the job, which shows that some women are still ready to sacrifice their careers if it is affecting their children and family which shows that the double burden often acts as a hindrance for their career development. It is the mother's role of a woman which cannot be substituted. But they are firm on their opinion about priority to job. Few respondents gave priority to their jobs, come what may they were not ready to compromise with their careers, that is an emerging trend.

Husband's co-operation due to the job

The increase in the number of employed women has modified their social roles. It has affected the traditional division of labour in the family. Women have acquired a certain amount of power by their contribution to the income of their family. Employment of women is also expected to have an impact on children and marital relations. The role of women has been undergoing alteration and expansion. On this point, Feldman states (1958: 54), "The working women represent more than a relatively new phenomenon. Now, the middle-class working wife is a potent economic, psychological, political and sociological force. Her newness, her numbers, her psycho-socio-economic impact upon the family and upon the society of which it is a part warrants examination". The husband's co-operation assumes great importance in the case of the working wife. A woman can carry on both the duties of housework and office work if she has the co-operation of husband, and other family members. Ross (1961) found in her study that two-thirds of the men interviewed favoured the idea of women's employment. But if the husband is not co-operative it leads to conflicts and quarrels in the house and sometimes not being able to cope up with the conflict and dual duties the woman has to give up her career and kill her dreams and aspirations.

So, in order to understand whether the respondents got the co-operation of their husbands, the following question was put to them, "What co-operation does your husband extend to you because of your job?" Majority, i.e., 244(61.9%) respondents said that their husbands were satisfied and they even encouraged them by sharing the children's responsibility, by helping in the housework, and also sometimes by boosting their morale when the respondents were feeling low due to office tensions. The respondents also said that the husbands gave them advice when needed about office problems. Only 11(2.8%) respondents said that their husbands were not happy with their jobs and it led to quarrels between them. Close to 91(23.1%) respondents were unemployed and the others 48(12.2%) although employed were unmarried.

One respondent's husband was telling her to leave the job as it was affecting their child. Another respondent earned more than her husband which hurt the husband's ego and so her husband was not happy and he always picked up fights with her on some excuse. Another respondent's husband was a well-known businessman and he did not want her to work as the husband thought that the job was not necessary. One respondent working as a Class II officer said, "Till both my kids reached the age of ten, my husband took the night shifts so that he could be at home from morning till evening with the kids. I am really grateful to him for his support". One more respondent working as an accounts officer said, "During audits, I have to stay late in the office due to workload, my husband cooks, feeds the children and puts them to sleep many a times, by the time I reach home. It is because of him that I have been successful in my job". Two respondents who held officer's posts in the excise department said, "Every morning it is our husbands who make tea for us. Sometimes when there are search parties we go home late. On such days the husbands manage everything at home".

The above data shows that majority of the respondents' husbands were happy, satisfied and even encouraged the respondents in their jobs by sharing the children's responsibility, by helping in housework, and even by boosting their confidence and advising them on their office problems, that is a significant change. Few of the respondent's husbands were not happy due to their wife's job as the husbands felt that the respondent's job was affecting the child, their ego was hurt due to the more income of the wife and they also felt that when the family is well off, the wife should not work. This shows that few men are still holding on to traditional attitudes regarding the employment of women.

Status of economically independent woman in relation to economically dependent woman

Status as a concept is used to denote a person's position in a social group and is relative to the status or position of other individuals and groups in the society. The status of a woman is intimately connected to her economic position. The society's development depends on the economic status of the women. It is seen that education and employment has improved the status of women not only in her own eyes but also in the opinion of the society. A number of studies such as those by Desai (1957) and Kapadia (1966) indicate that there has been a considerable change in the status of working women from their traditional status in present-day India.

In order to explore the opinion of the respondents about the status of an economically independent woman in the present study, they were asked, "What do you think, is the status of an economically independent woman in relation to an economically dependent woman?" It was observed that three-fourth, i.e., 298(75.6%) of the respondents replied that the status of an economically independent woman is certainly superior to that of the economically dependent woman. The respondents said that money had power and due to their earning capacity they enjoyed more power in the family. They felt that they did not have to depend on anyone for their necessities and this gave them a high feeling and confidence. While only 5(1.3%) respondents felt that the status of an economically independent and economically dependent woman was equal. All these five respondents were illiterate, married before the age of 18, and were now above 55 years of age. Maybe they still believed in the traditional belief that 'work for the man is to earn for the family' and the woman was supposed to look after the household duties and so they were not aware of economic independence.

Two respondents, one a teacher and the other a doctor said, "It is because of our employment and earnings we have a status in the family. We are involved in all decisions, big as well as small, in the family". A respondent running a beauty parlour said, "I earn more than my husband so it is possible for us to lead a better standard of living and give all the facilities to our child; he goes to one of the best and costly schools. All in the family respect me and I think it is due to my employment". Another respondent, an officer in government office, said, "While buying a flat, we took loan and my share is more than my husband so the flat is on my name. I have definitely got this status due to employment". While two of the uneducated respondents, one helping the husband in their vegetable shop and the other a chapatti maker in a mess said, "Women should work only if necessary, asking for money for running the house from the husband doesn't harm your status, it is his duty to earn for the house as it is our duty to look after everything and care for everybody in the house. Where is the question of status over here?

The analysis shows that a high majority of the women accept that the status of an economically independent woman is superior to that of an economically dependent woman and they feel that due to double incomes they have a better standard of living and can give their children all the facilities, that is an emerging trend which shows that women are trying to improve their socio-economic status. And a few respondents felt that the status of an economically independent woman was equal to the status of an economically dependent woman, they felt that there was no question of status and one should not feel bad to ask money from the husband as it was his duty to earn for the house as it was the woman's duty to take care of the household duties. This may be due to the fact that there is no awareness in them due to their illiteracy and early marriage. They were confined in the four walls of the house with a limited world view.

Opinion on women's employment

According to the traditional notion, women are expected to perform household tasks and it is for men to take care of outside work. It was undesirable for a woman to work outside and earn money as it was for the man to do household work. But due to recent socio-economic and political changes more and more women are taking up gainful employment and this has brought mixed reactions from both professionals and lay persons. Sociologists such as Bossard (1954), Lundberg and Farnham (1947) felt that the increased employment of women led to high divorce rates, more crime and that it was harmful to children. Many a people consider that the employment of women is the cause of many social problems.

In this context, the respondents in the present study were asked to give their opinion on women's employment. It was seen that almost three-fourth, i.e., 298(75.6%) respondents said that women should work. The responses were as follows: (1) A woman should work for financial security, independence and self-respect. (2) For the bright future of children in today's time of spiralling prices. (3) The respondents felt that career and family were separate issues and that housework problem can be solved by keeping servants. (4) Work is important for women's empowerment and one should not waste their education and talent by just sitting at home. (5) The respondents also felt that even if the financial condition of the family was very good, one should work for self-satisfaction. All the respondents felt that it is not necessary that a woman has to do an eight-hour job, she can do something from the home or take up a part-time job also by which she can get mental satisfaction and some money also, but she should not be doing only housework. And, only 5 (1.3%) respondents felt that a woman should not work because: (1) It would disturb peaceful family life and it would affect the children. (2) Working against the will of husband/in-laws/ parents led to marital/family tensions. (3) The respondents also felt that working women faced harassment in the office and that working made them less feminine and more arrogant. (4) Working women had no emotional security, no peace and no leisure. These respondents felt that women should work only under special circumstances if the need was there and if the family wished.

Two respondents said, "Today as the cost of living is increasing and if one wants to have a better quality of life, bright future for children and save for future plans as life itself has become unpredictable with no guarantee of job, marriage, health so women should also take up employment. Moreover work is important for women's empowerment because only if she has economic independence she can assert for her rights". Another respondent from a wealthy family said, "There is no economic necessity for me to work, but still I feel one should work for self-satisfaction, self-respect and one should not waste one's education by doing only housework. I work for a charitable trust where I teach poor children, the money I get is not much but I get satisfaction". Another self-employed respondent said, "It is not necessary for everyone to do an eight-hour job; sitting at home also one can do many things. The most important is utilizing one's time constructively and earn a little bit which is one's own". Three respondents felt that one should work only if necessary and if the husband and family wishes. They felt that the children and family get neglected, moreover a working woman had no leisure, no emotional security, she faced harassment in the office, became less feminine and so on.

The above data clearly shows that majority of the women favoured the idea that women should work as it was necessary for women's empowerment, to lead a better life, for self-identity, financial security, self-satisfaction, for utilizing one's time meaningfully and use of one's education. And a negligible percentage of the respondents felt that woman should not work as it created problems for the family, children and that a working women faced harassment in the office, she had no emotional security, peace and leisure and they felt that she became arrogant and less feminine. They said that only if the need was there and if the family wished one should work. On the whole, it is seen that women want to be economically independent and have an identity for themselves.

Economic Issues among Unemployed Women

Traditionally, women were homemakers and men were earners. The status of Indian women is in a process of change, they have more options open to them than in the traditional society of the past years. With the increased pace of urbanization and modernization, the educated women of all classes are gradually entering areas of activities and roles which were usually considered to be masculine. But it is seen that some of them still hold on to age-old traditions, values and customs. It is surprising that still many have objections to the idea of women working outside like in Gore's (1968) study of Delhi Aggarwal families where 43 per cent of them rejected the idea of women working outside and 33 per cent said that women might work under special circumstances. In order to understand the economic issues among unemployed respondents, the following three indicators were selected such as:

1. Opposition to taking up a job
2. Preference to part-time or full-time job
3. Opinion on women's employment

Opposition to taking up a job

Though women are entering the workforce in large numbers still some of them face opposition in many ways. Some well-reputed families do not allow their women to work as it might harm their status and social standing, some families feel that if a woman works it affects the children and that women become arrogant, they do not respect elders. Some parents do not like their daughters to run after jobs before marriage due to the fear that they might not get good proposals. So even if a woman wants to work they face oppositions in many ways. Sometimes may be the women herself is not interested to work, she is happy in her domestic work and so on.

In order to find out if the unemployed respondents in the present study faced any type of opposition they were asked, "If you have not taken up any job is it due to any opposition?" The data was collected from 91(23%) unemployed respondents. Only 2(0.5%) respondents reported that there was opposition to their employment by their parents. They said that their parents first wanted them to get married and then decide whether to work or not according to their husband's and in-laws' wish. Just 8(2%) respondents faced opposition from their in-laws as the in-laws felt that their work will interfere with the domestic duties, nearly 15(3.8%) respondents faced opposition from their husbands, as their husbands earned well. The husbands felt that their wives should concentrate on the children and the respondent's additional income was not needed. Only 9(2.3%) respondents did not take up a job as it was against their family tradition and they had to follow it. Close to 19(4.8%) respondents themselves did not want to do a job as they were married into well-to-do families and also due to the fear of neglect of home and children. And out of them 5(1.3%) were in the process of hunting for a job, while 16(4.1%) respondents were not qualified to get a job and due to early marriage they could not complete their education. And 17(4.3%) respondents were still studying.

In a group interview, seven respondents who were graduates said that their husbands and in-laws were against their doing a job, as two of them were in a well-to-do family, the husband and in-laws thought that their working might affect the children, their domestic duties and also harm their reputation. Three of them were themselves not interested in taking up a job as their husbands were earning well and they were happy with their household duties and due to the fear of neglect of children. Another two postgraduate respondents who were in a teaching job before marriage were told by their husbands to leave their jobs after marriage as it was against their family tradition. Four respondents said that due to their early marriage (before the age of 18) they could not complete their education and were not qualified to get a job. Two unmarried respondents, one a degree holder in law and the other a diploma holder in commercial art, said that their parents were against their doing a job as the parents felt that if they went for jobs, interacted with men, their reputation would be spoilt and that they would not get marriage proposals. The parents tell them that they could go for a job after marriage if the husband wished so.

The above analysis shows that still some women face opposition for doing a job. Few respondents faced opposition from parents, husband and in-laws due to various reasons such as fear of neglect of children, hindrance to domestic duties, family tradition and fear of losing the status of the family. In case of unmarried respondents, it was the fear of parents of not getting good marriage proposals for the daughters as taking up a job meant interacting with men. Few of them were married early so they could not complete their education and so no employment. And few of the respondents were happy with their household duties and did not want to go for a job. So, in the end we can see that still some of them are stuck up in age-old attitudes when it comes to employment of women.

Preference to part-time or full-time job

It is only recently that there has been an increase in the employment of women. But, however, it is seen that women are not seen as much as men in extreme jobs and on high posts. We have seen in the previous section, "Economic issues involved in employed women's development" that some women either prefer to work from home or take up some part-time job as it will not affect their family. Some studies like that of F. Ivan Nye (1949, 1952) have shown that part-time employment by mothers has a positive effect on the adolescent children.

So, in order to explore if given a chance would these unemployed respondents like to do something gainful they were asked, "If given a chance would you prefer – part-time job, full-time job, some work which can be done at home, no outside work at all". The data was collected from 91(23%) unemployed respondents. Around 24(6.1%) respondents said that they would prefer part-time jobs as one could devote time to the care of children and family, one also got time for rest and recreation. Nearly 21(5.3%) of them said that they would prefer full-time jobs as they did not like to sit idle at home and moreover they would have economic independence. All these respondents were educated well and were in jobs before their marriage. They had to leave their good jobs due to opposition from their husbands and in-laws. Only 10(2.5%) respondents did not like to work and were happy with their housework. While 19(4.8%) respondents said that they would like to work from home if they got some work which could be done at home as they felt they were used to be at home and they had doubts whether they could go out and work. And 17(4.3%) respondents were students still studying.

In the group interview, two of the respondents said that they got married as soon as they finished their graduation, then due to the family tradition they were not allowed to take up a job, but if given a chance they said that they would like to work from home so that their domestic duties and children would not be neglected and it would not be against the tradition also. Another four respondents said that they would prefer a part-time job as it will be convenient, their family life will not be disturbed and they will get time for rest and recreation. Two respondents said that they would prefer full-time jobs. One was a teacher in a convent school before marriage and the other was a clerk in a bank, they were told to leave their jobs by their husbands after marriage as their husbands thought it might affect the children and the wife's additional income was not necessary. These respondents felt very bad. They said that all those years they were busy in rearing their children, but now when the children had grown up they felt idle at home and also felt bad that if they would have been at jobs today they would have been high posts with good salary and a status. One more respondent said, "My parents were not so well-to-do but they gave me education up to postgraduation and after marriage my husband made me leave the job. Today my parents have health problems and my brother is not earning well, I feel like helping them. Though my husband helps them sometimes, he behaves as if he is doing a favour for them. If I had my own money I would have the right to spend it as I want. Then I would have not listened to anyone. Today I feel the parents give their daughter education, get her married, spend so much on her education and marriage and afterwards when the parents are in need, the daughter cannot do anything for them. Why it is so that the boy can look after his parents life long and the daughter cannot do it? So I think every girl should have economic independence and she should have the right to utilize her earnings in whatever way she wants". One unmarried respondent who had done diploma in interior designing and was at home for the last four years said, "My parents are against me taking up a job as they feel that it will spoil their and my reputation, they are in the process of looking for marriage proposals for me and they say that I can do a job if my would-be husband allows me but not till I am in my parent's place". Another four respondents, all graduates said that they are happy with their domestic duties and they are using their education to teach their own children. They felt that education is not only about earning, one can use education for the children, in running the house efficiently and so on.

The data indicates that few of the respondents would like to go for part-time jobs if given a chance as that will give them time for the children, rest and recreation. Some others wanted to take up full-time jobs as these respondents were well-educated, were in jobs before marriage but had to give them up due to husband's or in-law's opposition, now when the children had grown up they felt idle at home and were repenting for leaving their jobs. Some of the respondents were ready to work from home as they felt that they were used to being at home and so they were not confident of going out and working, moreover they could keep a watch on the house by working at home. While rest of them felt that they were using their education for their children, to run the house properly and so they were happy to be housewives. In all, the data clearly shows that women's employment is still not free from the notion of traditional sex roles and employment of women is closely related to her family and this shapes her attitude towards employment.

Opinion on women's employment

According to the traditional notion, women are expected to perform household tasks and it is for the men to take care of outside work. Women working out of their homes under economic pressures is not a new trend, but increase in women's employment due to the various socio-economic changes is a recent phenomenon particularly among educated women. But still some feel that women's employment has given rise to problems as Bossard's (1954) Lundberg's and Farnham's (1947) studies show showing that the increased employment of women leads to high divorce rates, more crime, marital problems and that it is harmful to children. Others such as Parsons and Bales (1955) do not regard maternal employment as having serious consequences because jobs women seek do not compete with father's role as wage earners.

In the previous section, we have seen the opinion of employed women on women's employment. Since the present study has also focused on unemployed women and the reasons for their unemployment, it was also necessary to find out their opinion on women's employment. So they were asked to give their opinion on women's employment. Around 67(17%) of the respondents were of the opinion that women should work and the reasons given by them for their answer were: (1) A working woman has financial security, economic independence, self-respect and own identity. (2)

The respondents also felt that double income is necessary for bright future of the children and that housework problem can be solved by keeping servants. (3) And that work is important for women's empowerment, education should not be wasted by sitting at home and above all a woman should work for self-satisfaction even if the financial condition is very good. (4) Working women's status at home is higher than non-working women as she brings money at home. Nearly 24(6%) respondents felt that women should not work and the reasons given were: (1) A working woman cannot pay attention to the children and family, working disturbs the family life, she has no emotional security and no leisure time. But her status is more in the family than the non-working women. (2) Working woman faces harassment in the office, becomes arrogant and less feminine. (3) But the respondents felt that if the need is there and if the family has no objection a woman should work.

Six respondents, three of them who had left their jobs due to husband's opposition, two unmarried respondents who were not allowed to go for jobs by parents, and one respondent who could not take up a job due to the family tradition said, "Every women should have economic independence, a working woman can face any situation confidently, she has a self-identity, a status in the family, she doesn't have to depend on her husband or family for her necessities, moreover in today's atmosphere there is no guarantee of anything – your marriage, your children, your health so if one works one has at least some kind of future financial security. If not a full-time job every women should do something other than housework for money as well as for self-satisfaction". Three of the respondents, said, "Women should work only if necessary under special circumstances, otherwise housework itself is a full-time job which keeps you occupied all the time, one can use the education to be a perfect housewife, a good mother and wife. And going against the family and husband disturbs the peace in the house. So if it is not necessary one should not work, as it will deprive somebody of a job who is more needy, but no doubt that working woman has more status in the family than non-working woman".

The data indicates that majority of the women were of the opinion that women should work as work gives a woman economic independence, financial security, an identity, self-respect, self-satisfaction, in addition to this working women's status at home is higher than non-working women as they bring money at home and it leads to women's empowerment. And all these things are directly leading to socio-economic development of the women. This shows that most of the women are aware of the benefits and consequences of employment, that is a significant change. While respondents were of the opinion that women should work only under special circumstances if necessary, as these respondents felt that housework itself is a full-time job and one can use one's education to be a perfect homemaker, and going against the family's wish for a job will disturb the peace of the house and moreover they felt that somebody more needy will be deprived of a job so in case of necessity only a woman should go for a job and they also were of the view that working women face harassment in the office, they become arrogant and less feminine with no emotional security, which shows that some women are happy with their traditional roles but they also feel that working woman has more status in the family than non-working woman as she brings money at home and it leads to economic and social development of the women.

Conclusion

Girl's education is a development imperative in India as it promotes social, economic and political progress among women and brings intergenerational benefits. From the foregoing analysis, a few conclusions have been drawn.

In the present study, it is seen that the aspiration for education is definitely higher among the respondents. Majority of them felt that girls should go for maximum possible education, they were ready to support the girls in any type of education, even in male-dominated fields such as army, navy, forestry, police and so on, they were ready to send the girls to hostels and wherever they got a seat of their choice. In addition to this, majority of them provided education to their daughters to seek employment and be independent, for future security and personality development. These can be said to be significant and emerging trends.

It is seen that nearly half of the respondents aspired for higher education, but only some of them were able to take up higher education and some could not due to reasons such as early marriage, financial worries, not getting a seat of choice, due to brothers and sisters studying. It is seen that even today girls are discriminated against boys with regard to education.

The data also reveals that even after many years of marriage, women aspire for higher education as in the present study few of the respondents went for higher education due to their own interest or to contribute to the family income or just for self-satisfaction. In few cases, the husband supported them by taking up some domestic responsibilities and that is a significant and emerging trend.

Almost all the respondents felt that the status of an educated woman is superior to an uneducated woman as she gets more respect and has a status in the society and family. The study also shows that majority felt that an educated mother is a better mother as she can educate the whole family and she has more skill in influencing her children. It is also found that the respondents took interest in activities such as going for admission of the child, enquired about the child's progress by visiting the teachers regularly, helped the children in their homework, which can all be said as significant changes.

Women's economic empowerment is absolutely essential for raising their status and which in turn will lead to their development in society. The women in the present study displayed a high participation ratio in economic activities. The number of women engaged in teaching and clerical jobs was highest, lowest being that of administrative jobs. Majority of the respondents were holding permanent jobs. Those who were helping the families and husbands in the business and all self-employed women were included in permanent jobs.

The data shows that majority of them were working on account of economic pressures and also to be economically independent, to have a status and to make use of their education. A large number of them were working to be self-reliant though they were financially well off, that is an emerging trend. The respondents were satisfied with their work as their seniors understood them, were helpful and co-operative, that is an important change. Even if some of the respondents had problems such as harassment at workplace, more work, night shifts and so on they said that financial independence is most important for them and working place and satisfaction are secondary to them, these are emerging trends. It is seen that few of the respondents were obeyed by their subordinates while few of them were resented as subordinates did not like to work under a female head but the respondents handled the situation well and brought everything under control, few of them were indifferent to a female boss which shows that men have started accepting women's superior position at the workplace that is again a significant change. Majority of the respondents revealed that they did not suffer any disadvantages due to their sex in the office and some who suffered disadvantages had been bold in tackling the sex bias at the workplace and that is a significant change and that shows woman is no longer weak and is ready to fight against discrimination.

The data regarding utilization of one's earnings shows that majority of the respondents contributed their salary to the family, some saved it for future plans, some gave part of the salary to their parents to help them financially or for their medical expenses with the knowledge of their husbands and that is an emerging trend. Few of them spent their earnings as they wished which shows that women are asserting their right in controlling their earnings.

In addition to this, the study also shows that some of the respondents believed that their working outside did not affect their children but it was seen that these respondents either worked from home or were self-employed or had a job where they could be at home when the children came from school. Some had a strong support system of their parents and in-laws. But it was seen that those who were holding jobs where they had to stay late or a job involving lot of stress the respondents suffered from guilt when they could not stay behind if the child was sick or when the children had exams and so on. This shows that a job is much more for a woman than cash benefits; it is closely associated with her whole life. In spite of all this, the respondents feel that they should have their own identity so they like to work, that is an emerging trend.

More than half of the respondents succeeded in bringing harmony between house and office as these respondents had fixed or flexible timings or they were self-employed. But some of them were guilt-ridden as they were in conflict due to dual duties especially when they had small kids. Though there was conflict the respondents were not ready to compromise with their careers, they were ready to work hard, make adjustments, as the job had given them their own identity, their own world and financial security. They gave importance to both housework and office work, come what may, they gave top priority to their jobs, that is a significant change and an emerging trend.

Majority of the respondents' husbands were happy and even encouraged the respondents in their jobs by sharing the domestic responsibilities, by boosting their confidence and advising them on their office problems, that is a significant change.

The analysis on status of an economically independent woman shows that a high majority of the woman accept that the status of an economically independent woman is superior to that of an economically dependent woman and they feel that due to the double income they had a better standard of living and they could give all the facilities to children, that is an emerging trend. In addition to this, the study also shows that the respondents favoured the idea that women should work to lead a better life, for self-identity, financial security, self-satisfaction, to utilize one's education and time meaningfully. They felt that these things directly lead to women's empowerment. On the whole, it is seen that women want to be economically independent and have an identity for themselves.

The analysis on opposition to work shows that still among unemployed respondents, some of the respondents face oppositions for doing a job either from parents, husband, or in-laws due to various reasons such as fear of neglect of children, interference in domestic duties, family custom and fear of losing the status of the family. In case of unmarried respondents, it is the fear of not getting good marriage proposals for the daughters as taking up a job meant interacting with men. It is seen that still some of them are stuck up in age-old attitudes when it comes to employment of women. The data also reveals that few of the respondents would like to go for part-time jobs if given a chance as that will give them time for the children, rest and recreation. Few of the respondents wanted to take up full-time jobs as they were well-educated, were in jobs before marriage and had given up their jobs due to husband's or in-laws' opposition, now the children having grown up, they felt idle at home and repented for leaving their jobs. Few of the respondents were ready to work from home as they felt that they were used to be at home and so were not sure of going out and working. While few of them felt that they were using their education for their children, to run the house properly and so they were happy to be housewives. In all, the data clearly shows that women's employment is still not free from the belief of established sex roles and employment of women is closely linked to their families and this shapes their attitude towards employment.

The opinion of unemployed respondents on women's employment indicates that majority of them held the opinion that women should work as it gives them economic independence, financial security, an identity, self-satisfaction and it leads to women's empowerment. This shows that most of the women are aware of the different aspects of employment that is a significant change. While few of the respondents were of the opinion that women should work only under special circumstances if necessary, this shows that some women are happy with their conventional roles. But they also feel that a working woman has more status in the family than non-working woman as she brings money at home and it leads to socio-economic development of the women.

4

Mass Media and Political Issues

This chapter concentrates on the mass media and political issues involved in women's development. The chapter is divided into two sections. The first section deals with role of the mass media in women's development and the second section concentrates on the political issues in women's development.

I

Role of the Mass Media in Women's Development

This section focuses on the extent of women's exposure to mass media and the role of the mass media in women's development.

Since post-Vedic period, patriarchal society came into existence. Social inequality and social discrimination have become the essential components of society. Traditionally, the Indian women existed because of the family and for the family. Margaret Cormack (1961: 178) writes, "The concept of the self becomes a negative one. She is the efficient server of the family, not thinking individual. It would be almost inconceivable for her to think of herself as separate from the family". Thus, she was a member of a group rather than an individual. C.A. Hate (1969) has pointed out that the status of women is definitely changing, more and more opportunities are coming her way, and she should grab them but yet her fundamental duty is towards her family – to make every member of the family a responsible member of society. But this was a limited view of the self. However, due to education and socio-economic changes, many women are coming out of the four walls of the home and the situation is changing. She is believed to have her aspirations, abilities and it is agreed that she should have the opportunities to develop herself. Thus, the woman has started caring for her cultural needs and interests, academic pursuits, social intercourse and so on. Our country has been engaged in planned development programme for women since long. But still it is found that we have failed in achieving the desired goals. Without making women aware of their rights and duties, and without obtaining their active participation, no plan of development can really succeed. It is here that the role of mass media becomes important for the development process. Exposure to mass media is an important variable in large-scale directed social change.

The important means of mass media are newspapers, television, radio and computer and so on. The means of mass media are significantly relevant to development. The function of the mass media is to open up the large masses of people to new information, new thoughts, new attitudes and new aspirations, create awareness and this in turn shapes the attitudes and beliefs of the people leading to development and new achievements. B. Kuppuswamy (1981) points out that even a man in a village is able to learn the other ways of living and other cultures than his own with the help of innovative communication. According to Daniel Lerner (1967), the educated people who are exposed to mass media develop a mobile personality with a capacity to identify themselves with new aspects of their environment. This movement is, by deliberate choice, due to new aspirations and thus a society consisting of such people may be called a mobile society. This is the reason why Lerner calls the mass media 'the mobile multiplier'. Pratima Kumari (1988) points out that the content of communication at any given time reflects the patterns of values of a society. For example, a subject dealing with the problem of women indicates the prevailing attitudes of the society towards its women and this can improve or lower women's status in the society by introducing new or interpreting old ideas.

In this section, an attempt has been made to study the extent of women's exposure to mass media and the role of the mass media in women's development. Keeping this fact in view the following five indicators were selected for the study:

1. Reading newspaper
2. Watching TV
3. Impact of TV programmes on women
4. Watching movies
5. Using computer

Reading Newspaper

The newspapers are a major aspect of modern educated and progressive society and is the most important media of mass communication. The newspaper is a swift medium for the delivery of news from the four directions of the world. It has played a significant role in highlighting the socio-economic problems, political issues, scientific and economic developments and a host of other issues concerning our day-to-day life. It has the potential to build or destroy any person or institution. A man can do without his breakfast but he cannot do without his newspaper. It is his first interest along with the morning tea. It is said to be the academic breakfast in urban areas. In the morning, women are busy in the kitchens in making breakfast, packing lunch boxes, sending children to school and so on. In spite of all this, the women go through the newspaper as soon as they find time. Till now reading newspaper was thought to be a privilege of elite women but now more and more women of educated middle-class in urban areas read newspapers with interest. It keeps them in touch with the events of the world and those of our country and states. The women are aware that if they want to claim political rights, contest elections, lead the nation and fight for equality, they should be well-acquainted with the news of the world. Preeti Kumari (2006) reports in the context of women, newspaper could not rank first because women have no time to go into details of the news and it is so because in India female literacy is at its lowest ladder but television has the honour of every section of society.

So, in order to see the respondents' exposure to newspapers, they were asked whether they read newspapers and if so how often? To this more than half (58.9%) of the respondents said that they read the newspaper daily while some (34.3%) of the respondents said that they read the newspaper sometimes and a few (5.8%) of them replied that they never read newspaper. Out of these respondents (1%) said that they do not get time, while (1.3%) of them were illiterate and (3.5%) of them said that they watched the news on TV.

In the group interview, two married postgraduate respondents who were housewives said that the day they do not get time to read the newspaper they feel as if they have missed something, but they make it a point to at least go through the headlines. One more respondent who is a graduate and housewife said that in the morning she goes through the headlines and either in the afternoon or at night she reads the whole newspaper in detail. Three respondents who were illiterate said that they watch Marathi news channel daily for the news. Two of the respondents working as domestic servants said that they come to know about the local news from different houses where they go to work. Four of the respondents said that newspaper is cheap and covers information from all areas.

The above data shows that more than half of the respondents read newspaper to get information on what is going on at local, national and international levels. They also said that newspaper covers information from all areas and is less expensive. A few respondents said that they never read newspaper as they do not get the time, some of them were illiterate and some of them said that they watched the news on the TV. The respondents also felt that the newspaper is less expensive and gives knowledge on all national and international events. It can also be seen that that the respondents are interested in getting news either through the TV or through friends or at the place of their work. In all, it can be said that almost all the respondents, whether literate or illiterate, are interested in knowing about the different happenings at local, national and international levels, which is a significant change.

Watching TV

TV has today become one of the indispensable necessities of life. Television seems to be the most effective and powerful electronic mass media. Television is basically an information dissemination source of development communication. Television provides entertainment to its viewers and also exposes them to socio-political and other events. It provides information about major national and international events. There are also programmes exclusively for women discussing their problems and giving them ideas on how to make use of their leisure time for economic gain. Such programmes are supposed to bring awareness among women. Of all forms of entertainment after a day's work and for relaxation there is nothing like an entertaining TV programme. A study conducted by Krishnan, Dighe and Rao (1986) on representation of women on Indian television indicated certain trends such as: (1) News related to women did not exceed 2.5 minutes out of the total 20 minutes. (2) In development-oriented news items, women featured as workers in tea plantations, sericulture, poultry farming, etc., and as beneficiaries of welfare schemes. (3) In women's programmes the focus was on the woman at home. (4) Where commercials were concerned, the lifestyles promoted were largely elitist; the models in the commercials were light skinned. Women were featured in all categories of commercials, but they were dominant in ads of foods, grooming and household items. (5) In voice-overs, male voices were presented as authoritative, female voices as informative and seductive. Kamalesh Mahajan (1990: 5) writes: "Women appear to have more fascination for television than men. In our society, males have outdoor interests also, but women have now found a glamorous source of indoor entertainment in the form of television. Obviously they are more attracted to it". Mridula Seth (1988) found that excessive viewing of TV resulted in negligence of study by both boys and girls; it has also resulted in their becoming unsocial and larger to have non-essential commodities. She also found some positive impact on students such as boys developed more sense of patriotism and co-operation while girls became aware of problems in society such as dowry, poverty, etc., information about rights and duties of women.

In the present study, in order to know the respondents' exposure to TV they were asked whether they watched TV. Almost all (78.7%) of the respondents replied that they watched TV regularly and some (19.8%) of the respondents said that they watched TV sometimes while few (1.5%) of the respondents said that they did not have a TV set so they watched it at the workplace when they had time. All these six respondents worked as maid servants.

In a group interview, eight respondents said that they watched TV regularly for news. Five respondents said that they watched yoga early in the morning and practised it. Eighteen respondents who were housewives said that they watched cookery shows and serials in the afternoon. Three respondents said that they only watched comedy shows as they were relaxing. Four respondents said, "The serials are boring and meaningless and they drag on for years. Children get spoiled and get wrong messages watching such serials". One respondent working as a reader in a college said that due to the cable network one is confused as to which channel one should see but it depends on the individual to watch the proper channel instead of blaming the media. Moreover, the media should be free from government control and have an autonomous status. Three respondents said, "Everything depends on the angle of viewing. If you view something from good point of view it will seem good for you, if you view it from bad point of view it will be bad for you".

The above data shows that almost all the respondents watched TV regularly and some of the respondents watched TV sometimes and few of them did not have a TV so they watched TV at their workplace when they had time. It is seen that the respondents watched TV for news, for working out, for cookery shows and serials. Some of the respondents watched comedy serials as they felt that they are relaxing, some felt that serials are boring and irrelevant and spoil the children. One respondent felt that one should know how to select and watch the proper channel instead of blaming the media. And some even felt that everything depends on the angle of viewing.

Impact of TV Programmes on Women

Today, a home is not supposed to be complete without a TV set. It has become a matter of routine to switch on the TV at the crack of dawn and keep it on till any programme continues. The impact of the TV programmes is such that even small children are getting affected and they ask their parents to get the things shown on TV. Men and women also are influenced so much so that they try to copy the style of their favourite characters. This media can thus contribute towards the development of skills and images in a society. It can assist change in attitudes by providing ideal models of behaviour and can raise aspirations. The success or failure of development plans in education, family planning, community development, health and nutrition depends on the involvement and participation of women. It is only through serving the interests of women that TV would be able to fulfil its role as a development tool.

So, in order to see whether the respondents agreed that the TV programmes had an impact on society and led to social change, the following seven indicators were selected:

1. Liberation of women from the shackles of custom
2. Development of knowledge
3. Knowledge of national and international events
4. Helpful in educational development
5. Helpful in health-related knowledge
6. Removal of caste consciousness
7. Eradication of dowry system

Liberation of women from the shackles of custom

Traditionally, women in our country seldom enjoy equality with men. The cultural background never allowed women to have space for themselves. Her life was only limited to family affairs and there too she had a subordinate place. But today the changing socio-economic factors have been the product and instrument for changes in the lives of women. Preeti Kumari (2006) reports that 25 per cent of her respondents agreed that TV programmes have liberated women from the shackles of custom.

In this context, the respondents were asked whether TV had helped in liberating women from the shackles of custom. Nearly half (41.9%) of the respondents said that TV has not helped in liberating women from the shackles of custom. Some (21.1%) of the respondents agreed that TV has helped in liberating women from the shackles of custom and some others (37.1%) held a neutral view on the impact of TV in liberating women from the shackles of custom.

In a group interview, three respondents who were well-educated and were working said that even today in many serials women are shown fully decked up with heavy make up who perform traditional roles such as keeping the husband's clothes ready, worshipping and fasting for the husband's long life, tolerating troublesome in-laws and so on. It is shown in such a way as if that is the way a woman should lead her life. Today, the woman is seen in all fields, successful in the office as well as at home, she should be shown as an independent and confident woman and also the way she manages things. But most of the time an economically independent woman is shown as smoking, boozing neurotic. Two respondents said that there are programmes which show women's achievements, how she succeeds and how she is proving her capabilities in male-dominated fields also. Seeing such programmes made them feel motivated and confident in doing things.

The above analysis shows that nearly half of the respondents felt that TV is not helping in liberating the women from the shackles of custom. They also felt that when women are proving themselves in all fields they should be presented as independent women having their own identity. While some of the respondents felt that TV is helping the women in liberating themselves from the shackles of custom. They felt that seeing such programmes on TV made them positive to do things assertively.

Development of knowledge

Television in recent times has nearly demolished the traditional forms of communication and has emerged as the most powerful and all pervading cultural force throughout the world. It provides information and latest developments from all over the world within a few minutes. Television plays an important role in educational development also. The government has started various educational programmes on TV. Various programmes are there for women too. Preeti Kumari's (2006) analysis reveals that maximum number of respondents agreed that TV helped in development of knowledge.

The respondents in the present study were asked whether TV helped in development of knowledge. Majority (77.2%) of the respondents said that the TV helped in development of knowledge while some (20.5%) of the respondents said that the TV did not help in the development of knowledge and a few (2.3%) of them took a neutral stand.

In a group interview, fourteen respondents said that there are channels such as discovery channel, history channel, NDTV and so on which help in development of knowledge. They also felt that even some serials and advertisements and films are helpful in education. If one sees the programme from learning point of view, it becomes educational. Three respondents said that TV did not help in development of knowledge. Today, most of the youngsters and kids watch reality shows most of the times and aspire to become rich and famous instantly. They are busy in sending SMSs to the organizers of the shows or are occupied with answering their stupid questions. And if they cannot make it to the shows it harms their self-confidence.

The data analysis shows that majority of the respondents felt that TV helped one in developing knowledge by watching channels such as discovery channel, history channel and so on and they also said that serials, advertisements also help in education if one views it from educational point of view, while some felt that TV is not helping in development of knowledge as today's children are busy watching reality shows, sending messages to these shows, or answering their questions so that they become rich and famous immediately and if they fail in it, it harms their personality.

Knowledge of national and international events

By its reach and impact, the TV provides a very powerful communication. In a vast country like India it is especially important as a medium of information and education. A mass medium is usually designed to reach a large, heterogeneous audience of widely dispersed people. Hence, people get knowledge about the national and international events. Information about national and international events is essential for a person to have an idea of the world and its country. In earlier days, newspaper and radio were the chief means of information about national and international events but because of illiteracy especially in Indian context women did not have access to print media. But now with the advent of television women have easy access to the information about national and international events. Preeti Kumari's (2006) study revealed that all the respondents accepted the fact that they gained information about national and international events through TV.

The respondents in the present study were asked whether TV had helped in spreading knowledge about national and international events. All (100%) of the respondents replied that TV helped in spreading knowledge of national and international events.

In a group interview, eighteen respondents said, "The dish antenna has revolutionized mass media, today we have so many channels and we get the knowledge of national and international events in minutes. If one doesn't get time to read the newspaper the TV is always there and it can be watched even while doing some work".

The above data reveals that all the respondents agreed that TV is helping in getting the knowledge of national and international events and they also felt that as there are channels in all languages even an illiterate can get knowledge of the events. It shows that women are interested in having information about national and international events.

Helpful in educational development

Initially, the role of TV was primarily directed towards programmes of entertainment. But it was felt that TV could not remain just a medium for entertainment but should include education. It was felt that TV should be utilized to disseminate information on science, technology, agriculture, health, as an instrument of social change. As children are human resources of the country, the TV should cater to both in-school and out-of-school education. Women and children make two-third of the total population so it is through serving the interests of women and children that TV would be able to fulfil its role as a development tool. The Committee on Status of Women (1974) observed that since formal education is costly and a long-term process it is essential to exploit the mass media for the eradication of illiteracy and to speed up the spread of education among women and girls. Preeti Kumari (2006: 95) says that Vikram Sarabhai was of the opinion that TV is one of the best mediums by which the educational development can be done even in remote areas.

The respondents were asked whether TV was helpful in educational development. Majority (77.4%) of the respondents agreed that TV is useful in educational development. Some (22.6%) of the respondents felt that TV is not helpful in educational development.

In the group interview, some 10 respondents said, "There are so many channels, but it depends which channel one is watching so that it helps in educational development. It is the parents who should control the children from watching irrelevant things and put the habit of watching educational channels in the children. Every technology has advantages and disadvantages but it is up to us to take up the advantages. Moreover programmes of television are educational in one way or the other but viewing angle is the prime thing for getting education from TV." Similarly, six respondents said, "TV has become a nuisance with all kinds of channels and programmes. Children have a tight schedule of school, then coaching classes, then some extra-curricular activities so after all this they do not get time to watch TV and whatever little time they get they sit and watch cartoon channels, so such channels should be presented an educative and interesting format so that the children enjoy as well as get some information from such channels".

The above data shows that majority of the respondents agreed that TV was useful in acquiring educational knowledge and they said that technology had its positive and negative sides and it depended on the viewer to watch meaningful channels and they also felt that parents should cultivate the habit of watching educational channels in children. Some of the respondents felt that TV was not helping in acquiring of educational knowledge, they felt that today children are engaged in routine studies so much that when they get time they watch cartoon channels only, so these respondents suggested that the channels watched by children should be presented in an informative and educative way.

Helpful in health-related knowledge

It is a historical fact that women in India occupy a lower social position. However, the situation is changing due to the changing socio-economic and cultural environment. Women are mostly confined to their homes and family or are engaged in looking after and caring for the family members. They have a habit of neglecting their health problems till they become serious. Some of the women are not aware of the symptoms of the disease and they just learn to live with it. Ignorance is high among the rural women. Mira Seth (2001) points out that the family planning programme is placing undue burden on women for contraception, over 96 per cent of the sterilization cases continue to be of women. Men's participation and responsibility for the control of family size has to be increased at all costs. The mass media can play an important role to inform and bring awareness among women in health-related knowledge. Preeti Kumari (2006) points out that almost all her respondents felt that TV was the most influential source of mass communication as far as health-related knowledge was concerned.

In this context, the respondents were asked whether TV was helpful in health-related knowledge. Majority (73.1%) of the respondents said that TV was helpful in spreading health-related knowledge and some (18%) of the respondents felt that TV was not helping in giving health-related knowledge and few (8.9%) of them gave no response to this question.

In a group interview, twelve respondents said that there are specific channels which concentrated on health issues and they also show solutions on health problems. Also, some programmes show exercises to improve one's health in general. In between serials advertisements are shown on AIDS, vaccinations, family planning, immunization and so on which are educative. Four respondents who were doctors and two respondents who were teachers felt that the channels which show exercises for certain health problems were not proper as it is necessary to take the doctor's permission to do such exercises since different people have different body compositions and different health problems. Instead of helping the patient such exercises may aggravate the problem. Any programme on health should give detailed information about the problem, the symptoms, and the cure of it, the diet, and the lifestyle a person should follow and so on. There are umpteen number of channels nowadays which guarantee to cure any disease and such channels are misleading and confusing the public.

The above data reveals that majority of the respondents felt that TV was helping in the development of health knowledge, they said that certain channels focused on health issues and suggested solutions and some exercises which were helpful to maintain health. They also felt that the advertisements shown on various diseases were educative and informative. While some of the respondents felt that the TV was not useful in development of health knowledge. According to them, a doctor's advice was necessary to carry out the exercises shown on TV otherwise the exercise might aggravate the problem as different people have different problems. They also felt that any programme focusing on health should do detailed and in-depth study otherwise it could mislead and confuse the viewers.

Removal of caste consciousness

Traditional India was characterized by a rigid caste system. But, the post-independence period witnessed urbanization, industrialization, spread of education, socio-religious reforms, growth of modern professions and growth of economy due to which the caste system no longer functions on rigid lines. But in spite of these advancements, one does hear incidences of caste inequalities.

The mass media exerts a strong influence on shaping the public attitudes. The mass media is so powerful and all pervasive that it is within their power to either stimulate or retard change significantly. Television can play a crucial role in creating awareness and generating public opinion in removal of caste consciousness.

The respondents in the present study were asked whether TV was helping in removal of caste consciousness. More than half (55.6%) of the respondents were of the view that TV has helped in removal of caste consciousness. Some (25.4%) of the respondents held the view that TV has not helped in removal of caste consciousness while some (19%) of the respondents had a neutral view on whether TV has been useful in removal of caste consciousness.

In a group interview, three respondents said that change can be seen in urban areas where people are going in for inter-caste as well as inter-religious marriages. People are not bothered about caste, there is inter-dining between all castes. People give more importance to class rather than caste; they like to move around with people of the same class for status. This change has been brought about by the mass media upto a certain extent. Five respondents said, "Though caste feeling is not found in urban areas, caste still prevails in villages and rural areas where inter-caste marriages are still opposed strongly, caste enmity still prevails leading to caste wars, sometimes even in cities there are caste riots. It appears that mass media has not been effective in removing the caste feeling as caste is rooted in the Indian culture and Indian tradition since thousands of years. Since the government controls a significant section of the mass media, it should set the pace and do something more. With government, the role of family is also important here."

The above data indicates that more than half of the respondents agreed that TV has been useful in removal of caste consciousness up to a certain extent as the change can be seen in urban areas in the form of inter-caste and inter-religious marriages. They also felt that more than caste, class determined one's status. Some of the respondents disagreed that TV has helped in removal of caste consciousness as caste is rooted in the Indian culture and Indian tradition since thousands of years. They felt that though the change is evident in cities there is still a caste consciousness in rural areas and villages where inter-caste marriages are not allowed and caste wars take place, even cities come across caste riots. They felt that the government should do more to remove caste consciousness as it controls a section of mass media. And, the role of family is also important.

Eradication of dowry system

In the ordinary sense, dowry refers to the money, gifts, goods or estate that a wife brings to her husband's house in marriage. The importance of the problem of dowry is to be assessed as cases of burning brides are increasing, a good number of girls remain unmarried due to parents' inability to pay dowry which is leading to social problems. In the last few decades due to industrial revolution, spread of democratic values, prevailing socio-economic environment has certainly changed the status of women, but still the custom of dowry continues because of the vested interests. The women themselves should stand up against this evil custom of dowry and in order to bring a change in mindsets and create awareness the TV can play a crucial role as the serials and programmes shown are the depiction of society, they can become agents of social change. Audiences can be acquainted with various social problems and ways and means of removing them. Preeti Kumari (2006) noted that some of the important serials were helping in removing various types of social evils. Dowry system has been supported by 43.78 per cent of the respondents of her study.

The respondents of the present study were asked whether TV had a role in eradication of dowry custom. Nearly half (47%) of the respondents replied in positive, they felt that TV is certainly helping in changing the attitudes of people with regard to the custom of dowry. And some (36.8%) of the respondents said that TV is not playing a role in eradication of the dowry custom. While some (16.2%) of the respondents did not have any reply on whether TV is helping in removal of dowry custom or not.

In the group interview, two students doing their postgraduation said, "Our parents are looking proposals for us, but we have decided that if the boy's family demands dowry we are not going to marry in that family. Few years back, an ordinary girl from Bombay had got the bridegroom and his parents arrested on the day of her marriage as they had asked for dowry. It was widely covered by many channels. When an ordinary girl can do it why not we? A time has come when we girls have to stand up against the dowry custom, even against the parents if they don't listen to us, then only the boy's and his family will get a lesson. There are many serials hitting the dowry system and these serials are creating awareness and putting courage among women". Three respondents who were of middle age and housewives said that even if one knows that it is against the law to give dowry, one has to follow it otherwise the girl remains unmarried and her family loses status in the society. The media instead of showing meaningless serials should concentrate on the social issues. One graduate respondent who got married recently was given a huge amount of dowry. She said that her parents were trying to get her married since last four years but good proposals were not coming and this proposal was good but they demanded a large dowry. She did not like it at all but was helpless in front of her parents. The mass media should first of all instil confidence in the minds of people so that they stand up against evil practices like dowry.

The above data shows that nearly half of the respondents held the view that TV was playing an important role in eradication of the dowry custom and there are some programmes shown which are inspiring young girls to stand up against the custom of dowry. There are some serials also which are dealing with the curse of dowry system and creating awareness among women. Some of the respondents felt that TV was not playing a role in removal of dowry custom; they said that one has to follow the practice due to fear of losing status in society and girls remaining unmarried. They felt that the media should show more programmes on social issues and should infuse confidence among the viewers so that the mindsets of people are changed, instead of showing irrelevant, meaningless serials.

The above analysis on the seven indicators shows that nearly half of the respondents felt that TV is not showing the women as having an independent identity and is not helping in liberating the women from the shackles of custom. Even today in many serials women are shown fully decked up with heavy make up and performing traditional roles such as keeping the husband's clothes ready, worshipping and fasting for the husband's long life, tolerating troublesome in-laws and so on. It is shown in such a way as if that is the way a woman should lead her life. Today, the woman is seen in all fields successful in the office as well as at home, she should be shown as an independent and confident woman and also the way she manages things. But most of the times an economically independent woman is shown as a smoking, boozing neurotic. Majority of them felt that TV is helping in development of knowledge through channels such as history channel, discovery channel, etc. All the respondents agreed that the TV is also helping in spreading the knowledge of national and international events. Majority of the respondents agreed that TV is useful in development of educational knowledge, health knowledge and more than half of the respondents felt that TV is helping in removal of caste consciousness up to a certain extent. They felt that it depended on the viewer to watch meaningful channels which give such messages and were educative and informative. A change can be seen in urban areas due to such programmes but much needs to be done in the village and rural areas. For some respondents mass media has not been effective in removing the caste feeling as caste is rooted in the Indian culture and Indian tradition since thousands of years. Since we have been brought up in caste culture; the role of government, the role of the family is important here. While nearly half of the respondents held the view that TV is playing a role in eradication of the dowry custom and there are some programmes and serials shown which are inspiring young girls to stand up against the custom of dowry and are creating awareness among women for the removal of social pathology. They felt that the media should show more programmes on social issues and should instil confidence among the viewers so that it changes the attitude of people, instead of showing insignificant and boring serials.

Watching Movies

The institution of cinema has occupied a position of far-reaching influence in the modern age. Movies are and will remain a major source of recreation; it reaches millions of people everyday, shaping their ideas, moving their emotions. It has gripped every class of people – upper, middle and lower. No form of recreation can compete with cinema offering maximum pleasure at minimum expense. Even small towns and villages have cinema halls. Films, like all cultural media, project a pattern of moral values as well as reveal traditional patterns. Influence of this media on social ideals and mode of behaviour is thus a two-way process. Pratima Kumari's (1988) study on graduate and postgraduate students of Patna University showed that 99 per cent of the respondents saw movies. Shashi Jain's (1988) study on middle-class educated and married women found that almost all the respondents were cinema-goers. Thus, it can be said that movies have achieved great popularity among women.

The respondents of the present study were asked whether they watched movies. Almost all (97.1%) of the respondents reported that they watched movies. They said that after a hard day's work, a visit to a cinema hall or watching a movie at home refreshes the spirits and chases away all boredom. A few (2.9%) respondents said that they never watched movies as they were not interested and felt that today's movies were not worth seeing.

In a group interview, 16 respondents who were all well-educated said that they liked to watch family-oriented or educational movies carrying a social message and not the typical commercial movies with song-dance sequences and violence. Three unmarried respondents said, "We like to watch romantic and comedy movies which are relaxing to the brain". Two students said that they liked suspense movies as they are thrilling and exciting. Four respondents who were in their fifties, three of them were housewives and one was working, said that they liked to watch only old movies which were calm and soothing to the eyes and ears.

The above analysis shows that almost all the respondents watched movies and most of them liked to watch family-oriented or educational movies with a social message. The youngsters liked to watch romantic and suspense movies as they were exciting while the older women liked to watch old movies as they felt that such movies were soothing. Few respondents were not interested in seeing movies and they also felt that today's movies were not worth watching.

Using Computer

The advent of computers and internet has revolutionized the concept of mass media. According to Lerner (1966: 71), "The mass media makes essential inputs to psycho-political life of transitional society via the minds and hearts of the people. It teaches people by depicting new and strange situations and familiarizes them with a range of opinions among which they can choose. A person becomes a participant by learning to have opinions. The more numerous and varied opinions the more participant he is". Today, most of the homes are incomplete without a computer. Cyber cafes are mushrooming every corner so that everybody has access to computers and internet. Even small kids are computer users. The internet plays an effective role in providing information and people are largely benefited by this.

In order to see the extent of the respondents' exposure to computers, they were asked whether they used computers. Nearly half (42.1%) of the respondents replied that they used computers for various purposes such as for getting information, for communication purpose, for storing data and for office work and more than half (57.9%) of the respondents said that they do not use computers as they had no knowledge of computers or they had no facility or it was not needed by them.

Three of the working respondents said, "Due to computers working has become easier. A large data can be handled by few people and any information can be retrieved by a single keystroke or by the click of the mouse". Another two working respondents said, "Although computers have made work easier after all it is technology handled by man and so it has its own disadvantages. If something goes wrong the whole data gets lost and work comes to a standstill, so it is always better to maintain written records also". One more working respondent said, "The internet is being misused by many and something should be done for it otherwise it is very useful". One professor said, "Nowadays students if given any project directly download it from the internet without understanding the concepts. Reading books is always recommended for understanding something and internet can be used as an aid to help oneself but depending totally on the net is harmful". One self-employed woman said, "I don't know why but I am lethargic to computers, only if it is necessary I sit on the computer otherwise I try to avoid it. Although I have an e-mail ID I use it only for professional use, otherwise I prefer to write to my friends and relatives, I think writing has a personal touch and individual style".

The data shows that nearly half of the respondents used the computers for various purposes as getting information, for storing data, for communication purposes; they felt that computers have made work easier. But they also felt that computer is a technology and if something goes wrong everything comes to a halt so it is better to have written records also. Some felt that the internet is being misused by many and that students are losing interest in reading books as they can download any information directly from the web which they felt is not a good habit. While more than half of the respondents did not use computers as they had no knowledge of it or they had no facility or they did not need it.

II
Political Issues in Women's Development

This section deals with the political issues involved in women's development by concentrating on the interest of the women in politics and the extent of their participation in politics.

In the traditional societies, political system and its control was the privilege of a few. In India, the participation of women in political activities and programmes is of recent origin. Till the end of the nineteenth century, women in India were under the evil customs like infanticide, child marriage and *sati*. They were economically dependent, socially weak and politically powerless. Three main indicators have been applied by the National Committee of the ICSSR to judge the political standing of women in our country: (1) participation in the political process as voters and candidates in election; (2) political attitudes such as awareness, commitment and involvement in politics and autonomy in political action and behaviour; and (3) their impact on the political process. According to Myron Weiner (1971: 164), "The concept of political participation refers to any voluntary action, successful or unsuccessful, organized or unorganized, episodic or continuous, employing legitimate or illegitimate methods, intended to influence the choice of public policies, the administration of public affairs, or the choice of political leaders at any level of government, local or national." In the past it was felt that politics was the exclusive domain of men but with the development of society, it was felt that women should be encouraged to participate in the political field. C.A. Hate (1969) reported that in the political field equality of sexes has not been achieved as the proportion of women playing a real part in political leadership is ridiculously small. There are hardly any women in the bodies which take political decisions and direct the state. According to her, women still have to fight against traditions and discrimination that hindered the realization of their political rights.

In order to see the actual interest of the women in politics and to know the extent of participation of the women in politics, the following indicators were selected for the study:

1. Voting behaviour
2. Consultation for casting the vote
3. Participation in canvassing, political meetings and agitations
4. Opinion on 33 per cent reservation
5. Membership in any association or political party
6. Attitude towards increased women's participation in politics

Voting Behaviour

Voting is the commonest yet the most important act of political participation. Women voters constitute an important component in any democracy. Till now women voters were not taken seriously. Illiteracy, preoccupation with household duties, looking after children, voting place far from their house were some of the reasons for low participation of women in voting. However, increasing awareness among women voters about their rights has begun to influence the political scene. In fact now there are large-scale efforts to woo the women voters. The "Doordarshan" telecast, 'Ankhon Dekhi' (1999) reported that the Chief Minister of Rajasthan has declared to build four lakh houses to provide shelter to widows. A number of schemes are also announced to woo women voters which reflects their importance.

The question of voting reflects the position of women in our democratic society. Adult franchise, declaring equality to all irrespective of property or rank is an event of worldwide significance. The political right to vote was granted to every adult citizen of India irrespective of sex from the time the Constitution became effective and the first free elections were held in politically free India. Voting is the basic means by which citizens are assimilated in the political process. Shashi Jain (1988) and Sanjay Ketan Jena (1994) and Inderjeet Kaur (1983) reported that women's participation in the voting process was very high.

In order to know the political awareness and participation of the women, the respondents were asked, "Do you vote?" The enquiry reveals that almost all (90.9%) respondents voted, except 21(5.3%) whose names were not in the voters' list, and 6(1.5%) were not voting due to change of address and 9(2.3%) who were not interested in voting. The respondents who voted said that it is the duty of every citizen and voting is a channel through which they can actively participate in politics.

In a group interview, six respondents said that they voted as it was the way through which they could show their support to their leader or party and that each vote is important in an election as it decides the fate of the party and so everybody should vote. Six respondents said that they had changed their residence and the place of voting was far so they did not vote in the previous elections, but now they were in the process of getting their names in the list with their new address so that they can vote the next time. Nine respondents said that they were not interested in voting as they felt that no matter which party wins, the condition will remain same. All political parties, which they said, are same with selfish motives and once they come into power they forget the promises they had made. Four respondents who were members of political parties said that they not only voted, but also paid house-to-house visits during elections, gave guidelines for voting to illiterate people and sat near the election booth and worked for the whole day.

Thus, it is seen that almost all women under study participated in voting which is a significant change compared to the traditional days. They are also aware that each vote is important as it decides the destiny of a party. Few respondents did not vote due to change of address but they were getting their names included in the new list, few respondent names were not in the voter's list and a few others were indifferent and did not vote as they felt that all political parties instead of working for the people had their own selfish intentions and make false promises.

Consultation for Casting the Vote

It is generally seen that in social matters a woman rarely exercises independent judgement. In a family, the woman willingly or unwillingly reacts to the actions and directions of some male figure in the family. The location of the polling booth, the distance of the booth from the house and the political climate around the polling booth are the factors seen by the male members before sending the females to exercise their voting rights. She is even told by the men in the family about who or which party to vote. She will not exercise her choice in most of the cases because she has never learnt to exercise her choice due to her submissive role, socio-economic dependence or lack of knowledge in decision-making. Shashi Jain's (1988) and Seema Salgoankar's (2006) studies revealed that majority of the respondents exercised their independent judgement in casting their votes.

So, to further investigate the voting behaviour of the respondents they were asked, "Whom do you consult before voting?" It is seen that none (82.5%) of the respondents consulted anyone and exercised independent judgement in casting their vote. And few (5.6%) were told by their husbands whom to vote while the other few (2.8%) consulted their friends and relatives before casting their votes.

Five respondents said, "There is no need to consult someone for a simple thing such as voting. We read newspaper, watch news and we are aware of the political happenings and we have knowledge of the various political parties so we know whom to vote". Two respondents said that their husbands worked for the BJP and during elections the husbands told them whom to vote for and they did as they were told. Three respondents said that they discuss about the various candidates and then they decide whom to vote.

Thus, it is seen that almost all the respondents relied on their own independent judgement for voting which shows that women have become politically aware. That is a noteworthy change. A few respondents had to listen to their husbands. It seems that these respondents considered their husbands as supreme and were stuck up in traditional values and others discussed with their friends or relatives before casting their votes.

Participation in Campaigning

In traditional India, mass illiteracy and a rigid social system cut off a great majority of women from effective participation in the political life of the country. Women's traditional role demanded full attention to the home, husband and family. They were expected to be submissive and docile. The social environment was such that it was not favourable for political participation.

However, with the removal of legal disabilities and with opportunities in education and employment, political awareness is increasing among the women. The technique of personal contact with the voters through political meetings, canvassing, holding agitations for demands imparts a personal touch and is more effective. Verba and Nie (1971) include various activities in campaign activity: (a) Persuade others how to vote. (b) Actively work for a party or a candidate. (c) Attend political meeting or rally. (d) Contribute money to a party or candidate. (e) Membership in political clubs.

Election meetings are an important medium for approaching the voters collectively to inform them about the party, its programmes, and its symbol and to introduce the candidate. Door-to-door canvassing on behalf of any candidate or party is also an index of commitment of the electorate. A proper and wide canvassing helps in mobilization of the voters. Seema Salgoankar (2001) reported that though the voting turnout was good, the interest and involvement in campaign activity was low as the meetings were usually held in towns where there was no proper transport facility, the meetings were mostly held at night so the time was not convenient for women, also the social taboos on the movement of women, lack of individual incentive are the reasons for non-participation of women in political campaigning.

In order to understand the degree of exposure of women voters to campaigning, the women were asked to inform whether they participated in campaigning, activities such as political meetings, election campaigns and agitations. It was seen that only a few (3.3%) respondents took part in agitations and political meetings. While some of the respondents (12.9%) took part in canvassing. It was seen that out of the thirteen women who participated in agitations and political meetings nine were from politically active families and two of them were corporators and the other two were members of BJP.

In a group interview, nine women who were from political families and four who were members of political parties like the BJP and Congress said that they not only participated in political meetings, but whenever the political leaders visited their areas during elections they arranged meetings to create political awareness and trust among people. Also, to spread awareness about their rights and the present political situation in the country, they also tell others to participate in political meetings. These respondents also said that not only they participated in agitations to show their support for their party, but they also convinced others to join agitations, bring awareness and change to a certain extent. Sixteen respondents said that they participated in the election campaigns for canvassing for their leader or party. They said they participated in the corporation, Vidhan Sabha and Lok Sabha election campaigns. Another four respondents said that they had distributed slips and pamphlets of their leader; had shouted slogans of their party, made house-to-house visits for canvassing and convinced others also to take part in canvassing. These respondents also took part in "padyatras" during elections not only in their locality but also in other localities. Six respondents said that they never took part in any political meetings, canvassing or agitations as they did not feel like doing so, they said that politics was not the field for women and they felt that everyone is selfish in politics and if one wanted to do something for the country one could do it without entering politics also. Three respondents said that their in-laws and husbands did not like them for canvassing because according to them women from good homes did not canvass or agitate on the roads, as it harmed the family status.

The above data shows that some of the respondents took part in canvassing, they distributed slips, pamphlets during elections, shouted slogans, and moreover they also took part in "padyatras" and convinced others also to join to support their candidates. In doing so, they created awareness among the people and sought their support. Few respondents took part in political meetings and agitations, but it was seen that these respondents' families had a political background; four of them were members of political parties. These respondents said that they arranged meetings during elections and also when a leader was visiting their area to create awareness, to give knowledge to the people about their rights. They also took part in agitations to show their support to their leader, to press for their demands and to bring a change in society. One interesting finding was that almost all the respondents exercised their voting rights but it was seen that when it came to actually participating in politics they were not so keen or interested in campaign activities as they feel that politics is a dirty field and is not meant for women. In some cases, their families feel that it will harm their status if their women went for canvassing or meetings or agitations. They are of the opinion that one does not have to serve the nation only through politics as there are many other ways to do that. On the whole, it can be said that though woman voters are increasing in number they are still traditional in outlook when it comes to real participation in politics. It seems domestic responsibilities, restrictions imposed by the family members and lack of interest are barriers in their path of participation.

Opinion on 33 Per cent Reservation

The position of women in society was very unsatisfactory as far as their social rights were considered. However, successive governments have concentrated on policies for women and tried to give them a place of dignity, equality and opportunity in a protected legal framework. Social legislation brings about reforms in the working of social institutions and the structure of any given society. Many acts such as the Hindu Succession Act, 1956, the Hindu Marriage Act, 1955, the Dowry Prohibition Act, 1961, the Maternity Benefit Act, 1961, the Equal Remuneration Act, 1976 and many more rights were given to women to improve their position in society. In spite of all these acts it is seen that women's position is not satisfactory, they continue to remain almost invisible in the power structures. This is due to the fact that there is underrepresentation of women in politics in India. On an average, women's representation in Lok Sabha from 1952 to 1956 has been 6 per cent and in Rajya Sabha it has been 10.3 per cent. There exists a large gap between representation and reality. The 73rd and 74th Constitutional Amendments have enforced 33 per cent reservation for women in local government only. There is demand for such reservation for women at parliamentary and assembly levels. Of course, there are women in politics but it is seen that they are 'proxies' which means they contest from a ward which is reserved for women. So, the women are just puppets and all the decisions are taken by the male members in the family. According to Seema Salgoankar (2006), who studied the political position of women "panchas" in Goa, reveals that women simply joined as dummies and for 21.2 per cent of them the decisions were made by the male family members and 33.3 per cent of them were influenced by the male members in the family in decision-making. Political parties are reluctant to give tickets to women candidates unless they are sure they will win. So the question arises whether women should organize themselves to demand more tickets for contesting elections or should there be reservation of seats for women. She also observed that majority of her respondents favoured reservation for women, which shows that if given the opportunity they are willing to have a say in decision-making.

In the above context the respondents of the present study were asked to give their opinion on 33 per cent reservation for women in legislative bodies. Almost all (80.5%) of the respondents were of the opinion that there should be 33 per cent reservation for women in legislative bodies and the reasons given for their opinion are: (1) women were oppressed right from the beginning so they need privileges for their upliftment; (2) as women should reach 50 per cent as fast as possible like men in all fields; and (3) for empowerment of women.

Some (10.5%) of the respondents were of the opinion that there should not be 33 per cent reservation for women in legislative bodies and the reasons given for their disagreement are: (1) women should attain equality based on their capabilities instead of asking for reservation; and (2) asking for reservation itself shows that women are inferior.

In the group interview, three respondents holding government jobs said, "Of course there should be 33 per cent reservation for women in legislative bodies as women are oppressed and suppressed even today and to improve their status, women should be there at the decision-making level and this is possible through reservation as parties will be forced to put up women candidates and it will be easier for women to fight elections." One respondent working as a maid servant said, "*Bayka baykanche paristhiti samajthat, bai varchya post la asli tar baikancha bhala honar*" (a woman can understand the problems of women so if a woman holds the post of decision-maker, women's position will become better). Two respondents, one an educated housewife and another a teacher said, "Today women are showing their capabilities and are excelling in all fields more than men. So why one should ask for reservation, asking for reservation itself shows that we women are weak and cannot compete with men. The experience of reservation in local bodies in some villages has already shown that the women members are mere puppets in the hands of the "sarpanch" husbands. Moreover, many women do not like to enter politics because of the increasing greed, conflicts, corruption and unholy competition. So there is a need to build confidence among people and change the opinion of people regarding politics and this has to be done by the government and our judiciary system". One respondent who is a professor said, "There are women leaders who are also corrupt and don't work for the masses. It is wrong to think that women will do a better job, if such women come through reservation, it will be of no benefit to anyone. Someone who is really honest and dedicated to work for the country irrespective of gender should be on the decision making level".

The above data reveals that almost all the respondents were of the opinion that there should be 33 per cent reservation for women in legislative bodies as according to them women are an oppressed lot and unless and until more or equal number of women as men are at the decision-making levels the status of women will remain same and as men do not want to lose their power they are not allowing the reservation bill to be passed. Reservation bill will be a means for women's upliftment, empowerment and development. They also said that a woman can understand women's problems well. While some of the respondents felt that there should not be 33 per cent reservation for women in legislative bodies as women have proved their abilities in other fields they should prove themselves in the field of politics also. They feel that by asking reservation, women are proving that they are weak and inferior. They also felt that the women who were elected through reservation in the "panchayat" were just dolls taking orders from the male members or "sarpanchs" and moreover due to corruption and controversies women think that politics is a dirty field. They suggested that it is the job of the government and the judiciary to change the viewpoint of people regarding politics. Some felt that irrespective of gender an honest person should be at the helm of affairs as it is seen that even women become selfish once they enter politics.

Membership in Any Association or Political Party

Traditionally, women have been a dormant segment in Indian society. Till recently they were only a unit of the family but now due to the various socio-political processes which have been at work since the early twentieth century, have made the woman a significant unit of the society. She has now become a leader, a social figure and an important instrument of social change. According to Hate (1969), the extent of women's participation in community life is the measure of social change in India. Seema Salgoankar (2001) in her study on women's political participation in Goa reports that only 6.6 per cent respondents are members of organization.

In any society women are victims of subjugation and aggression in varying degrees. This has led to coming up of a number of organizations working on multiple problems of women such as poverty, violence, health, dowry deaths and so on. Memberships to organizations or associations also indicate social participation. Organizations perform an important function of interest articulation. Membership or identification with a political party indicates a person's political thinking and beliefs. They take up various issues from time to time which have impact on elections.

So, in order to know whether the respondents of the present study were involved with any organization or association they were asked, "Are you a member of any association or political party?" If they were members of any association or political party they were asked to tell about the nature of work of the association. However, among the total respondents only 22(5.1%) of the respondents were members of some organizations and 4(1.1%) were members of political party – two of them were corporators and belonged to the Congress party and two of them were members of BJP.

Out of 22(5.1%) respondents, 4(1%) were members of "mahila mandals" and they worked for the upliftment of women such as giving loans to women on low interest for their economic development, 7(1.8%) were members of organizations working for children and women which gave shelter to orphans, taught poor kids and counselled them on various issues, there were two lawyers working for these organizations whose job was to counsel the women and update them with the legal procedures in case of any problem. And 2(0.5%) out of them were members of "bhajan mandali" and they were involved in religious activities such as organizing "Satsangs" and visits to religious places and 3(0.8%) were members of "mazdoor sangh"/labour union and were involved in taking the issues of staff or workers to the management and fighting for the labour demands. While 4(1%) of them who were doctors were members of doctor's association and they arranged for free check-ups for the poor and also gave lectures on health-related topics to bring awareness among the people and also undertook counselling.

In the group interview, two respondents working as clerks in an office and two self-employed women said, "We started the 'Mahila Vikas Mandal' some four years back, there are twenty members in it and we collected thousand rupees from each one and deposited the amount in the bank. The minimum amount given as a loan is ₹ 2,000 and the maximum amount given is ₹ 5,000. And, the interest rate is just two per cent. Till now five poor women have benefited from this – one has become a vegetable vendor; one makes pickles and 'papads', three of them have started a mess and give lunch boxes to office-goers. They have been regular in paying back. So if well-to-do women of the society come forward and do such things it will help many a poor woman to stand on their feet". Two of the doctors said, "We are members of Indian Dental Association and we organize lectures on dental issues to create awareness among the people about dental problems and we also organize free check-up camps every second and fourth Saturday of the month". Another doctor said that she worked for the Lion's Club and gave free consultation to the patients on every alternate day at the Lion's Club office. Two teachers said that they were members of 'Bal Shikshan Sanstha' and they took English classes free of charge twice a week. One of the respondents, who is a corporator, said, "I make use of my position to take up the issues of common man up to the higher level authority and try my best to find solution to the problems". Another respondent who is a housewife and is a member of the BJP said "Right from the beginning I am interested in social work, and I do a lot of social work in our area, seeing it I got the membership in BJP. Now I work for the party such as arranging visits of the leaders during elections, campaigning for the party and so on". Eleven respondents said that they did not like to work with organizations and neither were they interested in dirty politics. According to them, whether all these organizations were really genuine or not cannot be said so it seems they preferred to work on individual basis like helping someone poor directly, by donating food, clothes and even books directly to the concerned children, or by sponsoring a child's education and so on.

The above data indicates that none of the respondents were members of any association or political party and they preferred to work for the betterment of society on individual level as they had no faith in organizations and political parties. Very few respondents were members of some associations such as "mahila mandals", "bhajan mandals", "bal sansthas", labour unions and doctor's associations. These associations worked for economic upliftment of women by giving loans on low interest rates, some were involved in religious activities, and some worked for welfare of children and some of the organizations held free check-ups for the poor. The respondents helped these organizations by collecting funds, by teaching and guiding the poor children, by counselling the women on various issues, by telling them about the legalities in case of a problem, by arranging lectures on health-related topics, by organizing free check-ups and by organizing "satsangs" and visits to religious places. While few were members of political party, two of them were corporators and they solved the common man's problems by taking them to the higher authority and two of them were members who helped their parties by organizing meetings, by campaigning during elections and by creating political awareness among the people. Thus, it can be concluded that women's participation in organizations is very limited. It seems that tradition and family commitments still rule women when it comes to their social life and though it has started it will take time to gather momentum.

Attitude towards Increased Women's Participation in Politics

Women are more looked upon as members of the family rather than as individuals in our patriarchal society. Women are confined to home-bound activities and the role of mother, wife and daughter are seen as the natural roles for them. In these roles, most of their work goes unnoticed and it reduces her chances of wider participation in the economic, political or religious fields.

But, in recent decades, the country has been witnessing a change at the socio-economic front and a strong opinion is building up in favour of increasing women's involvement in the decision-making processes of the government. Reformers believe that if women come into power the entire political system would be transformed. It is claimed that female leaders, by virtue of their sex, would act as a cohesive force to bring about social change due to their innate qualities as being loving, caring, sharing and sensitive in handling problems. Revathi Narayanan (1994: 45) quotes Ella Bhatt, founder of SEWA, "Everywhere in the country we found the women were the most committed proponents of our future. So the future of the nation lies in the hands of these women".

It was, therefore, decided to analyze whether the increased participation of women in politics would lead to qualitative change in administration. The respondents were asked, "Do you foresee any qualitative change in administration with increased women's participation in politics?" Majority (63.7%) of the respondents agreed that increased women's participation in politics would certainly bring a change in the administration of the government and the reasons given for their positive reply were: (1) Nearly half (41.4%) of the respondents said that women's problems would be solved and it would raise the status of women. (2) Some (10.2%) of the respondents felt that people's faith in politics will increase. (3) Some (29.9%) of the respondents felt that it would lead to fast welfare of the nation. (4) Nearly half (47.2%) of the respondents felt that the nation's progress had to be achieved on individual basis by working with ethics and morals and it is not in the hands of politicians, whether men or women. (5) Some (33.5%) of of the respondents said that corruption would decline and would lead to clean politics. While some (36.3%) of the respondents answered in the negative, they were not of the opinion that increased women's participation in politics would bring a qualitative change in the administration and the reasons given for their negative reply were:

(1) Some (17.5%) of the respondents were of the view that whether men or women, politics would always remain same. (2) Few (6.6%) respondents felt that women were just puppets in politics dancing to the tunes of men as men were the main decision-makers. (3) Few (3.6%) respondents felt that the field of politics was not meant for women due to the increasing crime and corruption and it also tarnished one's image and character. (4) Some (27.4%) of the respondents felt that the nation's progress had to be achieved on individual basis by working with ethics and morals and it was not in the hands of politicians, whether men or women. The responses did not total up to 100 per cent as the respondents gave multiple responses to this question.

In a group interview, sixteen respondents said that increased women's participation in politics would certainly lead to qualitative changes, and make politics clean. Women are responsible for bringing up the next generation in the right direction due to qualities such as affection, hard work, patience, understanding, faithfulness and so on. These are the qualities a leader should possess to bring changes in society, so definitely with more number of women; the politics of the country will witness a qualitative change. According to these respondents, some women are corrupt but not as much as men, they said. Two respondents who were corporators said, "Women have a habit of getting into the depth of a problem and they handle issues sensitively so for any problem women will approach easily to a women leader as they have faith in her and this will make a difference. It will increase confidence among women and in turn will solve their problems and raise their status." Five respondents, all of them well educated and holding jobs, said that "Today politics is full of crime and corruption, everybody whether men or women are hungry for power and money. To get the power they use all possible means available and once they get it they use the position for selfish motives and forget the promises made to the public before getting elected. Even an honest person becomes corrupt once he/she enters politics as one has to go with the system otherwise he/she is thrown out of the system. So the nation's progress depends on an individual who has morals, ethics, dedication and devotion to work for the betterment of the country". Two of the respondents, one a housewife and the other self-employed said, "Politics is a dirty field. Once a woman enters politics she becomes a puppet in men's hands, she has to move around with men and this damages her character. It also involves a lot of money and muscle power so politics is not the field for women".

The above data indicates that majority of the respondents were of the opinion that increased women's participation in politics would bring qualitative change in administration, they felt that a woman has qualities such as understanding, affection, patience and sensitiveness in handling problems so with more women in politics corruption will decline, women's problems will be solved, the status of women will be raised and will lead to the welfare of the nation. While some of the respondents felt that politics is full of crime and corruption and that before elections the candidates make false promises never to be fulfilled, once they come into power by any means they become selfish. They also said that women are mere dolls in the hands of males and the main decision-makers are men, moreover when a woman enters politics her image is blemished so politics is not the right field for women. According to some, the nation's welfare is not in the hands of politicians but individuals with ethics, morals and dedication to work. In a nutshell, it can be said that women are inclined towards politics but are doubtful about the success of their participation due to traditional values on one hand and due to increasing criminalization in politics, also due to excessive use of money and muscle power on the other hand.

Conclusion

Traditionally, the fundamental duty of a woman was to the family, to take care of each member of the family. The concept of self did not exist for her. However, due to education and socio-economic changes many a woman is coming out of the four walls of the home and the situation is changing. Without making women aware of their rights and duties, without obtaining their active participation no plan of development can really succeed. Here the role of mass media becomes important as it can bring social change on a large scale.

The data analysis shows that more than half of the respondents under study read newspaper to get information at the local, national and international levels and were interested in knowing about the different happenings all over the world whether literate or illiterate that is a significant change.

Almost all the respondents watched TV regularly for news, for health knowledge, for cookery shows and serials. All the respondents agreed that TV was helping in gaining the knowledge of national and international events and they also felt even an illiterate can get knowledge of the events which shows that literacy is no barrier in watching TV. Some of the respondents watched comedy serials for relaxation, some felt that serials were boring and irrelevant and children were getting spoilt. The majority of the respondents felt that TV helped one in developing knowledge by watching channels such as discovery channel, history channel and so on. They also felt that some serials and advertisements were helpful in development of knowledge. In addition to this, it has been also found that TV is useful in development of educational knowledge and they also felt that parents should cultivate the habit of watching educational channels in children. Moreover they also felt that TV was helping in the development of health knowledge; they said that certain channels focused on health issues and the advertisements on various health issues shown were educative and informative.

Further, they argued that technology had its positive and negative sides and it depended on the viewer to watch meaningful channels and felt that one should know how to select and watch the proper channel instead of blaming the media.

The analysis on the impact of TV programmes on society as that leads to social change shows that nearly half of the respondents felt that TV was not helping in liberating the women from the shackles of customs. They said that when women were proving themselves in all fields she should be presented as an independent woman having her own identity, but instead she is shown in her traditional role. But they also felt that in some areas of social problems, TV was playing a crucial role as TV was helping in eradication of the dowry custom and was inspiring young girls to stand up against the custom of dowry, some serials were creating awareness among women in removal of social problems.

More than half of the respondents agreed that TV had been useful in removal of caste consciousness up to a certain extent as the number of inter-caste and inter-religious marriages was on the rise in the city though there might still be a caste consciousness in rural areas and villages where inter-caste marriages were not allowed and caste wars took place, even cities experienced caste riots. They said that as we have been brought up in caste culture, therefore, it is the responsibility of the government as well as the family to remove caste consciousness as it controls a section of mass media.

The data shows that almost all the respondents watched movies and most of them liked to watch family-oriented or educational movies with a social message. The youngsters liked to watch romantic and suspense movies as they were exciting while the older women liked to watch old movies as they felt that such movies were soothing.

Nearly half of the respondents used the computers for various purposes as getting information, for storing data, for communication purposes; they felt that computers had made work easier but as it was a machinery one should always maintain written records also to be on the safe side. Some felt that due to the internet students were losing interest in reading books as they could download any information directly from the net which they felt is not a good habit.

In India, the participation of women in political activities and programmes is of recent origin. In the past, it was felt that politics was the exclusive field of men but with the development of society, it was felt that women should be encouraged to participate in the political field.

It is seen that almost all women under study participated in voting which is a significant change from the traditional days. They were also aware that each vote was important as it decided the destiny of a party.

It is seen that almost all the respondents exercised their voting power with lot of independence and did not consult anyone on whom to vote which shows their political awareness and that can said to be a remarkable change.

The data on campaigning shows that some of the respondents who had a political background and four respondents who were members of political parties took part in canvassing, they distributed slips, pamphlets during elections, shouted slogans, took part in "padyatras", agitations and arranged meetings to make the people aware about their rights. One interesting finding is that though almost all the respondents exercised their voting rights, when it comes to actually participating in politics they were not interested in campaign activities as they felt that politics was a dirty field and was not meant for women and harmed the status of the family. On the whole, it can be said that though woman voters are increasing in number they are still traditional in outlook when it comes to real participating in politics. It seems household tasks, limitations imposed by the family members and lack of interest are the barriers in their path of participation.

Regarding reservation almost all the respondents were of the opinion that there should be 33 per cent reservation for women in legislative bodies because women are an oppressed lot and unless and until more or equal number of women as men are at the decision-making levels the status of women will remain same and the reservation bill will be a means for women's upliftment, empowerment and development and they felt since a woman understands the problems of women better, therefore, she should hold the post of decision-maker. Those who did not favour reservation felt that a woman should come up on her capabilities and they also felt that the women representatives who come through reservation were just dolls taking orders from the male members of the "panchayat" or "sarpanch". They suggested that the government and the judicial system should work to change the viewpoint of people regarding politics. Some felt that irrespective of gender, an honest and dedicated person should be at the helm of affairs as some women also became selfish once they got power.

The data on membership in organizations reveals that very few respondents were members of some associations such as "mahila mandals", "bhajan mandals", "bal sansthas", labour unions and doctor's associations which worked for economic upliftment of women by giving loans on low interest rates, welfare of children, organized free check-ups for the poor, some were involved in religious activities, updating the women about the legalities in case of a problem, arranging lectures on health-related topics, organizing "satsangs" and visits to religious places. While few respondents were members of political party, two of them were corporators and they solved the common man's problems by taking them to the higher authority and two of them were members who helped their parties by organizing meetings, by campaigning during elections and by creating political awareness among the people. Thus, it is seen that women's participation in organizations is very limited. It seems that the women's social life is still ruled by tradition and family commitments, though it has started it will take time to gather momentum.

Majority of the respondents were of the opinion that increased women's participation in politics will bring qualitative changes in administration, they felt that with qualities such as understanding nature, affection, patience and sensitiveness in handling problems could make women good leaders and with more women in politics, women's problems would be solved, would raise the status of women and would lead to fast development of the nation that is a significant change. While some of the respondents felt that whether men or women once in power they became self-centred. They also said that the main decision-makers were men, moreover when a woman entered politics she became a mere puppet and her image was blemished so politics was not the field for women. In a nutshell, it can be said that women are interested in politics but are doubtful about their success due to traditional values on one hand and due to increasing corruption, criminalization and muscle power in politics on the other hand.

5

Case Studies

With the intention of acquiring in-depth knowledge into the various aspects of the study, six typical case studies were done.

Case A

Mrs A is 53 years' old, a doctor by profession and has two children – a son doing his MS abroad and a daughter studying medicine. Her husband is an engineer and has his own business.

In her opinion, education is for the all-round development of the human personality – physical, intellectual, mental and emotional. The education of women is very essential for a healthy and happy home. Education is the only key which opens the door of life for women in the society. It can improve women's thinking and judgement, develop determination and self-esteem. Linked with education is economic power. Women should be economically independent so that they may prove their importance. Besides education, skill development programmes should be introduced according to the interests of the women such as flower production, fashion designing, preparing spices and so on. Special need-based schemes should be formulated for enabling them to set up their own projects. These schemes should be properly executed and marketed at all levels. Knowledge plays an important role in the empowerment of women. Without empowerment of women, the nation cannot progress fast.

Working women work outside the home while at the same time do a larger share of work than men at home. In some cases, as the husband and the family members are reluctant to help their wives. Thus, male dominance is a major hindrance faced by women in discharging their duties and the level of participation among women in all fields is low. Even in case of unmarried girls, it is mostly the fathers who take all the decisions. She feels that women are equally responsible for their condition; they suffer because they are silent and adjust themselves to any situation. They are afraid of the society, but she should not care for such criticism and go ahead.

A change in attitude is a must for women empowerment. There has to be a change in the people's mindsets and perceptions then only a new situation will develop. A mother should bring up her son and daughter without any discrimination; she only can lay the foundation for attitudinal change. A girl should be given all the resources and opportunities as a boy. They should be given freedom to take their own decisions, and then only they will have real equality with men.

Case B

Mrs B is 38 years' old and a teacher by profession in a private school, her husband is an architect and has two sons studying in school and stays in a joint family.

She says that traditions in the families affect the capabilities of women as they cannot lead and express their ideas and views in front of others. She says that no woman can succeed without help and a strong support system and women's dual duties affect their health, unless her husband and family members help in domestic work. When asked about decision-making at home she said that her husband and she herself take all the decisions jointly. She feels that even today women are successful in the teaching profession than in the other fields and she holds women responsible for their situation because they bear atrocities on themselves without a word of complaint. She is of the opinion that education can bring awareness among women about their rights and duties towards themselves and the media can play a vital role in this.

The government should try and provide vocational training to women to enable them to find employment and when they will be economically independent, they will become more self-confident in doing things and in taking decisions. It is seen that girls still face discrimination so the government should implement programmes relating to all-round development of the girl child. Education is one of the most important means of empowering women with the knowledge, skills and confidence required to participate fully in the development process.

Cultural attitudes towards women play a significant role in hindering their political participation. Merely giving women a few seats in politics is not enough but women have to work equally with men in the social and economic sphere. She asserts that woman need real power and real rights for themselves, which can be accomplished only when developmental plans are formulated and implemented by them. They should be given freedom to take decisions, and then only they will have real equality with men. She said only education, economic independence, and change in attitude and thinking can eradicate cruelties against women. In the end, she said that no country can achieve the goal of development without integrating the feminine factor into development.

Case C

Mrs C is 52 years' old, a graduate, and a social worker, has been involved in social work since 19 years and now has been elected as a corporator of Pimpri Chinchwad Municipal Corporation. Her husband is a government servant. She has two daughters, one is working as a teacher and the other is a clerk in a bank.

A daughter of village headmaster and teacher she was always interested in the upliftment of women belonging to the lower strata of the society. She is of the opinion that women should work continuously for the betterment of the society without caring for the criticism and comments of others.

She is of the opinion that tradition and culture do not affect anyone's capabilities but it is the mindset of the society and the person. According to her, self-confidence is the way for empowering oneself. Women must become aware of legal requirements.

She feels that education is a prerequisite for any kind of development; it is a must for every citizen, be it a male or female and should be made compulsory up to tenth standard at least for every child. She feels that due to reservation of women in local bodies, the confidence and capabilities in women have increased. She says that there should be reservation for women in parliament, state assemblies and government jobs, so that they can play a primary and participatory role in the development programmes. She is of the opinion that since half of the electorates are women, there is a need for political parties to attach importance to the women's issues. She says laws are already there, but implementation and enforcement are inadequate. Women nowadays are showing their capacity in all fields. Development cannot be sustainable unless and until people including women participate in the development process. If a nation has to prosper, it should include women in every aspect of life. Women have shown their capacity and they should be given the opportunity to work at all levels, make decisions at all levels without any pressure which will induce confidence in them and raise their aspirations.

Non-governmental organizations can play an important role in bridging barriers between women and the rest of the society, as they work at the grassroots level and interact closely with women at the village level.

She is of the opinion that a daughter has to look after her parents in their old age and should have equal rights in the property, should be allowed to perform the last funeral rites. She feels that it is high time that women should stop succumbing to social pressures. It is high time they gather courage to break the barriers of tradition and take an independent stand. Only then can the empowerment of women be considered complete.

She strongly supports 33 per cent reservation for women in legislative bodies. She feels that the government should take action to promote equal participation of women and provide equal opportunities for women to participate in all activities at all levels of decision-making. Till then, the empowerment of women holds little meaning and significance in their lives.

Case D

Mrs D is 46 years' old, is a postgraduate and an accounts officer by profession in a government office. Her husband is a manager in a private firm. She has one daughter doing BDS.

She says that education is the base of all developmental processes. It is one of the most important means of empowering women with knowledge, skills and development process. Women's dependency is the major obstacle in women empowerment. If a woman is independent of her financial sources, she has the power of money, then she will have more power in decision-making in the family as well as outside the family. So first of all financial freedom is a must for women empowerment.

Mostly in families, the mothers are responsible for differentiating between girls and boys. Tradition often determines that women should confine their interests to the domestic sphere, should not compete with men in work. The status of the girl child in our country can be measured by the rate of girl child mortality, by the declining sex ratio, their accessibility to health services and education. So to empower the girl child, it is necessary to bring awareness in the family before bringing awareness in society. There is a strong need for attitudinal change among men as well as women of our society. Women on their part should never regard themselves as weaker than men.

She also holds the opinion that women have poor representation at the parliamentary and legislative levels and that women's participation in politics is necessary for holistic development as women are bound to have a better viewpoint on matters such as education, healthcare and surroundings, particularly of the girl child, as these affect them directly.

She says that the psychology of the parents and the nature of Indian society is responsible for the attitude of girls choosing their career as a teacher, as a nurse, as a clerk, as a receptionist in particular after graduation, but cannot go for jobs such as conductor, driver, postman, soldier and policeman and they cannot take up those jobs which a male can take to earn a livelihood. First and foremost, it is the responsibility of the parents, the society and the government at large to ensure that the female child is allowed the freedom to educate herself in the field of her choice and also choose a career of her liking.

She said that both she and her husband take all the decisions jointly in all matters. In her view, a couple should have one or two children whether a boy or a girl. According to her, a girl should be married at the age above 26 and boys around 30 years, as both are matured, have completed their education and are settled in a career by this age.

She is a member of an association working for orphans. She is of the opinion that a small bit of social service by everyone in the society will make a huge difference over a period of time.

Case E

Mrs E is 56 years' old, principal of a reputed school, her husband is an income tax officer and has two daughters, one a doctor who went for inter-religious marriage and the other a fashion designer.

Talking about tradition she said that tradition need not be regressive. Practices such as 'purdah', child marriage, dowry system, marriage within the same caste, rituals practised during the time of marriage carried importance for that time period only and should not be practised in the present context. Tradition means creating a healthy social atmosphere. The values, beliefs which are modified with the changing times, should be considered traditional social values and beliefs.

Earlier girls' education was restricted and due to fear of foreign invaders parents married their daughters at a young age, but today parents are educating their daughters at par with their sons, encourage their daughters to take up jobs for financial security and an identity and so the marriageable age is increasing. Every practice was situation-specific and now those practices cannot be justified on the grounds of tradition. Modernity means change from within and not on the exterior front. There is no dividing line between tradition and modernity, it is a continuous process.

She is of the opinion that despite the spread of education, the families still continue to be traditional with regard to inter-caste marriages, mate selection and dowry. She said, "I supported my daughter to marry a boy of her choice even outside our religion.

People criticized me for such a thing, but one has to change with times". Change has to start at the individual level and then it will spread to others bringing an attitudinal change which will lead to development of society. Adapting oneself to the changing times is greatly needed.

She held the view that every woman should be economically independent as they have their own identity, status, financial security and above all mental and self-satisfaction. Security net for woman is education; economic empowerment, health and judiciary, the family, the society and the nation – the right mindset, and support of all these organizations is needed. But above all is the girl child's family's love, support and attitude which goes a long way in giving her the confidence needed to step out and live a dignified life.

She is of the opinion that all the siblings should have equal property rights of whether a girl or a boy and then it depends on him/her to accept it or not. According to her, it is the responsibility of the daughter to look after and take care of her parents. She said that her own parents come and stay with her for months as her brother is not so well-settled financially. She said that her family is responsible for her present position.

In the last, she summed up saying that women should develop their confidence level and increase their self-reliance to decide and determine their important choices in life. Power has to be acquired, exercised and preserved. Unless women themselves become conscious of their subjugation and oppression, show proficiency and grab the opportunities, it would not be possible to change their status.

Case F

Mrs F is 46 years' old, a lawyer by profession, and is also into social work. Her husband is a builder. She has two sons studying in eighth and sixth class.

Talking about the Indian society, she says that the lives of Indian women have been restricted by do's and don'ts regarding dress, their activities, education and role and so on. The issue of development arises only because women are still marginalized. The discrimination originates before the birth of a girl and is continued throughout her life. India is said to be 'Bharat Mata', and also due to its agricultural economy, land is associated with women in the form of 'Bhumi Devi'. But in spite of these honours women in India are viewed as 'Second Sex'. Barbaric practices such as female feticide, female infanticide, child labour, child marriage, rape, dowry, molestation, forced prostitution, gender inequality still continue to haunt women. They are powerless and do not have control over resources and hence little or no decision-making power.

She is of the opinion that education is a powerful tool in the development of women as it helps women to gain knowledge and it provides them the necessary courage and inner strength to face the challenges of life, to supplement the family income, to achieve social status, in empowering them. Though women are getting educated, the perception of women's education is still backward. Girls are still socialized to be a good wife, good mother and not for a challenging career. Though there has been a general all-round development, crimes against women have become a general feature. Education should promote new values which expose gender inequalities and injustice.

According to her, economic independence is a major means of developing women. In India, labour force participation of women is very slow. The general opposition towards women's employment, responsibilities at home, women's work and earning being treated as subsidiary to that of men, lack of adequate training and opportunities, absence of facilities such as childcare centres and safe transport are some of the factors which hinder female employment.

She is of the opinion that political empowerment is one of the most important elements in the overall empowerment of women as it gives women the capacity to control the decision-making process. She supports 33 per cent reservation for women strongly. Even after decades of the grant of political equality, statistics show that there is gender equality at the voter level, but within the power structures there is no gender equality. Even today, most of the women are uneducated, have little or no property and live in a tradition-bound society. In such cases, the politically powerful make them contest elections for their own gains. Majority of the women are not politically conscious due to lack of information and political awareness and they make their choices on the basis of suggestions from the male members of the family. Very few women have access to the core of the power structure and as a result they are left on the margin of political process. There is a need for greater positive action to raise political consciousness from the 'panchayat' level to the state and national level.

She also said that legislation is an important instrument of social change but it cannot be carried out in isolation. Legal equality without social and economic equality is meaningless and women have been exploited in the name of religion and tradition. Awareness and knowledge about women's rights to equality have to be created among women and also in the society. Women should also become aware of their legal rights and demand their fair implementation. In addition, she is of the view that women themselves should be involved in the judiciary in a much bigger way as judicial officers, lawyers or police.

Lastly, she said that it is not enough to empower women through education, employment and participation in decision-making. There should be cultural and social empowerment of women. There should be attitudinal change; principles of justice and equality should be ingrained in the minds of each and every individual in the society. There is a need for creation of awareness for achievement, to search for one's identity and this can be done through means of communication, media, government and non-government organizations.

6

Summary and Conclusion

In this study, the issues involved in women's development with reference to Maharashtrian women in Pune, have been analyzed. Specific investigation on how issues of socio-cultural, educational, occupational, and political and mass media play a role in women's development has been done. In order to get empirical evidences about the issues involved in women's development in Pune, questions mentioned in Chapter 1, were explored using the concept of development.

As Pune city is characterized by cultural, educational, military, religious and industrial features, the city was selected as a research area for the study.

The important areas and suburbs of Pune city such as Pune station, Aundh, Shivajinagar, Kirkee, Pimpri, Yerwada, Nigdi, Bhosari and Chinchwad were selected for the study. Purposive sampling method was used, where participants were selected with known characteristics. A sample of 394 women was selected for the study.

In issues, the present study has focused on decision-making process in the family among married women, their opinion on certain deep-rooted customs and practices in Indian society and their attitude towards social participation. It has also focused on decision-making among unmarried women with regard to their freedom in certain things in day-to-day life, their involvement in the family decisions and their opinion on important decisions of their life. As the socio-cultural issues for married and unmarried women are different and the present study consisted of 73.1 per cent married women and 21.3 per cent unmarried women. In addition to this, the study has also focused on role fluidity such as their opinion on male/husband doing housework such as how far the family members of the respondents share the housework, and also their attitude regarding some traditional beliefs and duties towards the husband and family, and lastly on their attitude towards property rights of women.

The present study on Maharashtrian women of Pune has shown that in majority of the respondents, both husband and wife take decisions jointly regarding education of children, financial matters, shopping for major items of the house, visits or picnics, and number of children, that is an emerging trend. In nearly half of the respondents, women's opinion is also given weightage in decisions such as settling marriages and emergency expenses and both husband and wife take decisions. While when it comes to decisions regarding kitchen matters and shopping for daily items it is still the women who make decisions in majority of the cases which indicates that kitchen and cooking is still thought to be the field of women. In decisions regarding buying and selling of property and mate selection, it is the male members in the family who take decisions in nearly half of the respondents. On the whole it is seen that important money-centred decisions such as buying and selling of property and mate selection decisions which have far-reaching importance are taken by the husbands or male members of the family due to the feeling of male superiority. The thinking that woman is not inferior to man can be seen in the changing nature of the authority structure in the family where women are now participating in large numbers in decision-making and that is a significant change.

Their opinion on certain deep-rooted customs and practices in the Indian society shows that nearly half of the respondents show an increasing ambition towards career and want to settle in a career before marriage, as it will give them financial independence, more status and confidence in doing things and that is a noteworthy change, and only (2%) of the respondents are focusing only on marriage. And though most of the respondents had no choice in their own marriage yet half of the respondents were ready to give freedom to their daughters to select their mates which indicates that parents are becoming more understanding that can be said to be a new aspect of the changing socio-cultural atmosphere. Some of them were rational as they said that it depends on the situation.

The analysis indicates that three-fourths of the respondents held a negative attitude towards the custom of dowry which seems to be a healthy change. They felt that dowry is the worst custom in society responsible for female and low status of women and as women are equally earning and showing her capabilities in all fields as men, the dowry custom should be wiped out from the family level which will bring a change in society and would lead to development and empowerment of women. It is observed that some of the respondents brought dowry at the time of their marriages. Some got dowry in gift form and some in cash form. In the case of some, dowry was demanded. So again, it is difficult to say whether in practice the system of dowry will continue or end because though majority of the respondents had a negative attitude towards dowry, whether it will be practised by them cannot be said.

More than half of the respondents under study felt that the ideal number of children is two as they feel that the children learn sharing, caring and develop a helping nature and they will not be self-centred. Moreover, they did not make any discrimination between the sex of the children and they just wanted a healthy child when they were expecting the first child. And also felt that a family is complete even without a boy, that is a significant attitudinal change. The data also points that some respondents still want one male child out of the two children to carry the family name forward, to have a status in society, for material and spiritual advancement, to support parents in old age, to perform the last rites of parents and to achieve 'moksha'. Few of them preferred a son due to fear of in-laws and husband as they felt that girl child is a responsibility; a lot has to be spent on her marriage in the form of a huge dowry, and parents cannot depend economically on their daughters which shows that the practice of discrimination exists even now. While few of the respondents wanted only girl child as they felt that the girls understand and love their parents, there is no difference between girls and boys, and girls are as good as boys in all fields today and nowadays even boys do not stay with the parents. It is a myth that sons take care of parents in old age, which is a progressive change. One interesting point to be noted is that few respondents felt that for balance in the sex ratio a family should have a son and a daughter.

But in spite of these significant changes, one thing that has not changed is that even now the number of women undergoing family planning operation is very large compared to men who are reluctant to undergo this operation due to fear that it would affect their vigour and vitality. It can be said that traditional attitudes are still holding some men from undergoing vasectomy.

In the present study, more than half of the respondents feel that there is nothing wrong in performance of the last rites by daughters, as girls and boys are equal and both have the same blood running in them. Moreover, they feel that today girls are seen in all fields and they are no longer weaker; they can bear the scene of any of their parents' funeral, and they also said that if one has no son then the daughter should be allowed to do the funeral rites and that is a significant and an emerging trend. While some of the respondents were against the opinion of daughter performing funeral rites as they feel that it is against our religion and tradition, as she is no more a member of the family after marriage and also because girls are emotionally weak to be able to see the last rites of their parents and also due to the fear that the soul will not attain 'moksha', that shows that tradition and religion still play an important role regarding a daughter performing funeral rites.

The data regarding discrimination of food as compared to the brother shows that majority of the respondents were not discriminated, which is a noteworthy change, but few of the respondents were discriminated in this matter like the brother got food first and whatever he demanded like milk or any special dish. Though the percentage is very small, this shows that girls are still discriminated with regard to food as compared to boys.

With regard to taking meals it is seen that some of the respondents had their food according to the situation, some with all the family members, or with their husbands. That is a significant change compared to the earlier days when women were supposed to eat after serving all the family members. Regarding the practice of eating leftover food, the data indicates that almost all the respondents do not follow the practice of eating leftover food which shows that the practice of eating leftover food alone by the women is definitely changing.

The data regarding the attitude of the women towards social participation reveals that nearly half of the respondents visit their friends' houses singly or with their husband and family members, more than half of the respondent's husbands and family members had no objection to the visits of the women to a friend's house and majority of the respondents were free to talk to their husbands' friends. It can be said that attitudes are changing towards the socialization of women. These are some emerging trends and it can be seen that the respondent's husband and families are progressive and they allow the respondents to have a social life of their own.

The data on membership to socio-cultural organizations shows that few of the respondents were members of chit fund, NGO and 'bhajan mandali' at the society/residential areas. More than half of the respondents were not members of any organization. Those who were members, of them few of the respondents were involved in the socio-religious, cultural activities in their residential areas, while few of the respondents were doing social work through NGOs or in residential areas, whereas few of the respondents organized kitty parties and picnics at the society/residential areas and few of the respondents organized visits to religious places. And a negligible number of the respondents were involved in other activities such as helping the poor, teaching the poor children at individual level. So it can be concluded that women's participation in associations or mandals is limited. Even today women are not participating in voluntary organizations. It seems that the traditional restrictions regarding women's family duties and family life are not allowing women to be active members of organizations.

The socio-cultural issues among unmarried women regarding decisions with respect to freedom in day-to-day activities, show that almost all of the respondents were given freedom to go to movies, majority of the respondents were free to move alone, but at the same time the parents kept an eye on the respondents like who were their friends and the respondents were not supposed to stay out late in the evenings, not go for late-night movie shows and so on. Almost all the respondents respected their parents and did not take any decisions without their parents' knowledge though the parents had given them freedom. This shows the changed attitude of the parents towards the movement of girls and their friendship with boys and also the girls' relaxed attitude towards the boys. This may be due to increasing education and awareness that the attitudes of the parents are changing, and the restriction towards the free movement of unmarried girls is decreasing but at the same time the data shows that the freedom had certain limitations.

As for involvement in family decisions among unmarried women, as far as shopping for the family and for the respondent is considered almost all the parents like to take their daughters' opinion and all the respondents are given freedom regarding shopping for the family and shopping for their requirements, but regarding family finances few of the parents felt that the respondents are young and not mature enough to be burdened with family finance matters and that they should focus on their education and career. It is also seen that the respondents respect their parents, give credit to their opinions, rarely think of opposing them and they never take any decision without talking and consulting with their parents and the parents also do not try to impose the traditional ways on the respondents.

The data on important decisions of life among unmarried respondents shows that majority of the respondents want to be settled in a career before marriage as they will have financial independence, more status and confidence in doing things. They also felt that personal growth is not possible after marriage as it puts extra burden. Few of the respondents said that one should get married first as marriage gives stability, makes life disciplined, and satisfies biological, psychological and social needs. They also said that as one's age increases getting married becomes difficult and one can decide about career according to the circumstances. They felt that both marriage and career are important and both should happen at the right time. A negligible number of the respondents felt that only career is important as marriage is an unnecessary headache and if one is settled in a career she can face any situation even if unmarried. It is clear that attitudes towards marriage are changing, as the respondents feel that in today's changing environment marriage does not guarantee security and happiness. Only one respondent said that only marriage is important while two respondents felt that only career is important. That shows an emerging trend to remain single. The employed women no longer regard marriage as necessary for financial support or for self-respect. There is a growing honesty about the brittleness of happiness in marriage.

Regarding continuation of job after marriage, it is seen that almost all the respondents said that they would like to work after marriage, as job will give them an identity, economic independence and will help in the bright future of the children if both of them worked. The respondents also said that the housework problem can be solved by keeping servants. They feel that education should not be wasted by sitting at home and work is important for women's empowerment so they said that even if the financial condition is very good they would like to work. Few of the respondents said that it depends on the situation and the financial condition of the future family in which they will get married. If the husband and the family are against their working they will not work. The data indicates that the respondents are conscious of their own identity, individuality, economic independence; at the same time they are aware of the fact that today due to increase in prices, two incomes have become necessary to maintain a certain standard of living and they want to maintain it by working and earning.

The data on the type of marriage the respondents would like to have shows that nearly half of the respondents wanted their parents to select the groom but also felt that their consent should be taken before finalizing the marriage. Some of the respondents said they would like to go for love marriage as it is necessary to know about the life partner before marriage but even if it is love marriage the parents should approve it. Some of the respondents felt that love marriages do not succeed so they would go for arranged marriages. Two of the respondents wanted to remain unmarried showing an emerging trend to remain single. Hence, it can be concluded that arranged marriage is still predominant and most of the respondents wanted their parents' approval in any type of marriage.

The data regarding the age for marriage, it is seen that some of the respondents felt 21 to 25 years as the right age to be married. And most of the respondents preferred the age of 25 to 30 years as appropriate marriageable age as they think completion of education takes at least 22 years and another 2 to 3 years to settle in a career and by this time one is mature enough to take important decisions about her life and also about marriage as it is the most important happening in one's life. That is a significant change in attitude which shows that the respondents consider the woman as having an independent identity.

Regarding the traits in the choice of husband, it is seen that majority of the respondents gave topmost priority to education, then occupation and then preference to emotional and mental compatibility of the boy. It is interesting to note that in India endogamy is prevalent but present study shows that caste is not important for today's generation. It reflects a social change from the former days when a boy from a well-reputed family from the same caste holding a respectable position in the community was sought for.

The data on the number of children the respondents would like to have after getting married shows that half of the respondents said it would be one child for them as in today's situation only one child could be maintained satisfactorily. Some of the respondents wanted two children as they felt that two children were needed to learn the values such as sharing and caring. Few of the respondents said that they have not thought whether to have one or two kids or they might not like to have children at all, which is an upcoming trend. It is seen that attitudes regarding the family size are changing and most of the respondents want to restrict their family size to one or two children. And few of the respondents are not sure whether to have children or not. The respondents also said that children are a great responsibility and if one cannot do full justice to the children than it is better not to have children. That is an emerging trend.

The data on the changing trends in dressing pattern shows that all the respondents felt salwar kameez, saree and churidhar kurta is good as it suits the Indian culture, it is modest, gives a comfortable feel and can be worn by women of any age. An interesting point is that three of the respondents felt that saree is bad as it is exposing. Some of the respondents felt that jeans with long tops is good as it is not exposing, gives a comfortable feel and can be worn by women of any age. Few of the respondents said that jeans with short tops is good as it is today's fashion and gives a smart look and few of the respondents held that low waist jeans is good as it is today's fashion, is comfortable and compels one to remain slim. Few of the respondents approved that mini skirt is good and looks good on teenagers. They also said that any dress can be worn but one should know how to carry oneself confidently and it depends on individual wish. It is seen that tradition still rules with regards to dressing pattern, as most of the respondents preferred salwar kameez, saree, churidhar kurta and jeans with long tops while few felt that jeans with short tops, low waist jeans and mini skirts are good as they give a smart look.

It is also seen that nearly all of the respondents were restricted by their parents from wearing mini skirts and most of the respondents were restricted from wearing low waist jeans and some of the respondents were prohibited from wearing jeans with short tops. Three of the respondents who were students said that they themselves do not like to wear dresses such as mini skirts, low waist jeans and jeans with short tops. The respondents were restricted to wear such dresses because of the tradition and social, religious ethical and moral values. This shows that parents still want their daughters to wear traditional dresses such as saree, kameez, churidhar kurta and jeans with long tops because of their social, religious and moral values.

As for data regarding role fluidity between husband and wife or male and female, almost all the respondents said that husband and family members should share household work. They felt that if a woman can manage both house and job then why not men? As a life partner, husband should do 50 per cent of the housework. The respondents also felt that seeing the father doing housework, the son will also learn to do it and that woman and man both have complementary roles to play in society and no one is superior or inferior. The respondents were of the view that if the woman is working the husband should do 50 per cent of the housework and if the woman is a housewife the husband should do at least 25 per cent of the housework. Almost all the respondents were of the opinion that the males should do household work and that is a very significant change and only few of them did not appreciate men doing housework and felt that males doing housework is against our custom.

Data on the husbands helping in the housework clearly shows that those who help in the house undertake those assignments which are considered less awkward for them such as dusting, shopping for grocery and taking care of the children. The fact is that the major responsibility of doing most of the housework within the four walls of the house is still on the women.

The data regarding family's help when the respondent falls sick indicates that some of the respondents are helped by the husband, servant, children, in-laws and relatives when they fall sick. It is seen that housework is shouldered mostly by the husband and also by the family members when the respondent is not well that is a notable change.

Data regarding son's help in housework shows that some of the respondents' sons helped them in the housework like their daughters. Many of the respondents held the view that boys should know everything from cooking to washing, because for education or a job they have to go to different places away from the family, moreover both the spouses are working nowadays and when girls can earn and be independent then why can not boys do the housework? It shows that the respondents themselves have socialized the sons and daughters equally without discrimination which can be said to be a promising development.

The data on the attitude of the women towards their husbands shows that majority of the respondents felt that a wife has equal status as that of her husband. The interesting point to be noted here is that majority of them no longer consider their husbands as superior but they do believe in superior and inferior status of husband and wife. There is an emerging thought as some of the respondents feel that relation of husband and wife is complementary.

The women's attitudes regarding some traditional beliefs and duties towards the husband and family clearly show that though the respondents consider some of the duties like giving tea and serving hot food as fine, but they are not ready to perform duties such as keeping the clothes ready, not giving leftover food, polishing his shoes, the husband as the respondent thinks such duties are humiliating. Also the respondents no longer like to keep quiet if the husbands scold them for no reason and no longer like to obey their husbands if they are wrong. Again almost all the respondents said that they believe in doing some of the traditional duties sometimes just out of love for their husband such as keeping his clothes ready, not giving him leftover food and so on. But they made it clear that they should not be compelled to do the duties as everyday work. This clearly indicates that though the women believe in some of the duties they are not ready to perform them routinely as in the older days that shows their assertiveness.

In the context of a woman looking after her parents, majority of the respondents said that the woman can look after the parents both in financial and emotional matters even after marriage because the respondents feel that if a son can look after his parents, it is the daughter's duty to look after them as the parents educated her, got her married and moreover today girls are equally showing their capabilities in all fields as a boy and time has come when the traditional practices should be given up. Some even said that if the girl is earning she should give half salary to her parents and the parents should stay with the daughter also as they stay with the son. This shows that there is an attitudinal change and girls are ready to take the responsibility of their parents. Few of the respondents said that a woman should not look after the parents after marriage as the husband and in-laws may not like it. Moreover, if the parents are well-settled, they do not need help of the daughter. The parents themselves do not like it and if the woman is not an earning member then it creates problems in her own family. Some of the respondents felt that it is fine to look after the parents but in certain limits otherwise it leads to problems in their married life.

Data on women's attitudes towards property rights of women, and giving equal right to women in father's property, reveals that majority of the respondents are in favour of the legislation as they feel that both sons and daughters are equal and as a legal heiress, the daughter should be given her share of property. Some were not in favour of the present legislation giving equal rights to women in father's property as they felt that a lot has to be spent on the daughter's marriage along with the dowry. As she inherits property from her husband's side, she should not ask for share in parental property. And, a negligible number of the respondents felt that only in particular circumstances, like if the daughter is in need, she should be given a share in parental property.

The data on possession of property reveals that more than half of the women were not in possession of any property. Those who had, mostly had a share in the husband's property, some of them had acquired property through their own efforts and few of them had got it in dowry, from their father and in-laws and a small number got it as a gift from relatives.

The data regarding implementation of property rights reveals that though the respondents were aware of the legislation of equal rights in property there was not a single respondent who got an equal share in the property as the brother and they were satisfied with whatever little they got, but were not ready to fight it out legally, as they felt that it will spoil their relation with the brother and their paternal family which shows that women are not bold enough to stand for their rights and they give up when it comes to relationships and family.

In the educational issues, it is revealed that the women under study attached great importance to education. The data shows that majority of the respondents aspired that women should get higher education and parents are keen on educating the girls in areas in which the girls are interested and areas which are thought to be male-dominated, that is an emerging trend.

The data regarding the level of education advocated for girls reveals that majority of the respondents wanted girls to get maximum possible education, that is a significant aspect. One noteworthy point today is that leaving the traditional fields such as medicine, engineering, teaching, the respondents are aware that one can make a career in offbeat fields also if one has interest and the parents are ready to support their daughters in any type of education, that is an emerging trend.

Though the respondents themselves were not sent to hostels, more than half of the respondents were ready to send their daughters to a hostel if they get a seat of her choice, that is a very significant change. But they feel that the girl should be trained in such a way that she can handle any situation and for that she should be made mentally and physically strong. Some of them were not ready to send their daughters to hostels, this shows that traditional attitude and restrictions regarding girls are still present.

It is seen that the purpose of getting the children educated falls in two categories, i.e., personal and social. It is found that majority of the parents provide education to the daughters mainly to be economically independent, to make their future secure in today's changing environment, for knowledge enhancement and personality development. Few of them gave education to their daughters to seek good husbands and that is related to personal interest. While some of the parents educate their daughters as it leads to empowerment of women that eventually leads to national development and also due to the thinking that if one woman gets educated the whole family gets educated, that is related to social interest. In all, the main reason for getting the girls educated is economic independence and future security.

The data regarding higher education reveals that nearly half of them aspired for higher education which shows that women's aspirations for education are definitely becoming higher but only some of the respondents were able to take up higher education while some could not go for higher education due to financial worries, opposition from parents for marriage, due to discrimination between son and daughter. Few of them did not secure a seat and a negligible number of the respondents had to give up their dreams of higher education as their sisters and brothers were pursuing higher education.

Data on education after marriage indicates that women aim for higher education even after many years of marriage and few of the respondents were themselves interested in going for higher education for mental satisfaction, in few cases it is the husband supporting the wife and encouraging her to go for higher education by helping her in domestic responsibilities, that is an emerging trend. And few of them took up education to supplement the family income which shows that if a woman wishes to do something then age is not a barrier to her.

The data on the status of educated woman shows that almost all the respondents are of the opinion that an educated woman is of superior status in relation to an uneducated woman as she gets respect, has a position in the family and society, and her advice and opinions are sought in important issues, that is a significant aspect. While few felt that being educated is not enough and that to get superior status one should be dedicated to the family, give respect to the elders and do one's household duties perfectly, that shows that few of them still have traditional attitudes towards the role of woman.

The data on whether an educated mother is a better mother reveals that majority of the respondents feel that an educated mother is a better mother as she can guide the child in his/her studies, has more skill in influencing the children when needed and that is a significant change and some of the respondents feel that a cultured mother is more important than an educated mother for the all-round development of the child.

The data regarding participation in school activities shows that majority of the respondents went for admission of the child; prepared the child for the interview to get admission in a reputed school, that is a noteworthy change. The respondents took the time and went to meet the teachers regularly and also attended the parent-teacher meetings to know about the child's progress, that is a significant change. More than half of the respondents helped their children in their homework and took special care of the child during the exams, the working mothers took leave during the exams to guide the child, to give him/her moral support and in case the child was absent he/she was made to complete the missed notes and homework with the help of friends.

The economic issues are divided into two parts, first focuses on economic issues among employed women and second concentrates on the economic issues among unemployed women.

The women in the present study display a high participation ratio in economic activities. The data was collected from 303 (76.9%) working women. The working women were employed in a wide range of occupations – ranging from professional to unskilled. Women engaged in teaching and clerical jobs were highest, lowest being that in administrative jobs. Majority of the respondents held permanent jobs. Those who were helping the families and husbands in the business and all self-employed women were included in permanent jobs.

The data regarding the reasons for working shows that majority of the working women were in employment due to economic pressures and also to be economically independent, to make use of their education and to have a status. And few worked (a) to help their parents with their husband's knowledge, (b) due to the wish of their parents/in-laws/husband, or (c) to get away from the monotony of housework and make use of their time meaningfully. An interesting point to be noted here is that majority of them worked to be self-reliant though they were financially well off, that is an emerging trend.

Data on satisfaction with work shows that majority of the respondents were satisfied with their work as their seniors were helpful and co-operative, that is an important change. Few of them were not satisfied with their work as the job was not suitable to their qualifications, due to more work given by the seniors, mental harassment, non-appreciation of work, tiredness due to dual duties of housework and office work, night shifts and temporary jobs which show that some women are still not satisfied with the work conditions.

The data reveals that when the respondents are at a senior position in the office, the subordinates obey them, while few of the respondents were resented by their subordinates as they did not like to work under a female head but the respondent's way of handling the situations at work impressed the juniors and they started respecting the respondents, this shows that woman can be good managers and leaders. Few of the respondents reported that their subordinates were indifferent to their being a woman boss, that is a significant change and shows that men have started accepting women in senior positions at the workplace.

The data regarding disadvantages due to sex reveals that majority of the respondents did not experience any disadvantages due to their sex, as their colleagues were helpful and supportive, that is a significant change. And some of the respondents suffered disadvantages due to their being a woman like mental harassment, no support from the male colleagues, getting more work and no leave when required. But an interesting point to be noted is that the respondents have dared to confront sex bias situations at the workplace that shows that the women are no longer timid and are ready to fight against inequity on account of sex.

Data regarding utilization of one's earnings reveals that majority of the respondents contributed their salary to the family, some of the respondents saved some part of the salary for future plans which shows that the women are becoming smart, some of the respondents gave some part of the salary to their parents with the knowledge of their husbands to help their parents financially or for their medical expenses, that is an emerging trend. Few of them spent their earnings as they wished as their families were doing well, that shows that the working women are asserting their own right in controlling their own earnings. But at the same time, it is seen that some of the respondents still had to hand over their earnings to their husbands and in-laws that shows that male control still prevails in the society with regard to women's earnings.

Data regarding the effect of working on children clearly shows that some of the respondents believed that their working outside did not affect their children, but it is seen that most of these respondents were working from home or had a job or were self-employed where they could be at home when their children returned from school and so they were able to give time to their children. While those who were holding eight-hour jobs had their own ways of handling this problem by keeping servants or telling the neighbours to keep a watch or by keeping the children busy in some classes or some activities till they returned from the office. Though they are guilt-ridden at times, they felt that woman has to have her own identity. While some of the respondents felt that their working outside affects their children, they felt guilty when the children were sick, during their exams when they needed their mother the most. This shows that women always blame themselves and are torn between professional aspirations and family responsibilities, but at the same time they want to have their own identity, that is an emerging trend. This shows that a job for a woman is closely integrated with her whole life.

Data on harmony between house and office shows that more than half of the respondents have been successful in bringing harmony between the house and office due to their fixed and flexible timings as most of them were either self-employed or worked from home, may be so they could adjust their timings according to the needs of the family and children. Some of the respondents who were holding high-end jobs had a strong support system of their parents and the husbands. But some of them were facing a conflict and suffered from a sense of guilt as they could not bring harmony between the house and their job, as most of them were in professions where they had to stay late in the office, so the families and the respondents felt that the family and children were being neglected and were finding it difficult to carry on both the tasks especially when they had young children.

The data on giving priority to housework or office work shows that majority of the respondents would never think of leaving their jobs in the event of a conflict, but were ready to work hard and make adjustments, and that is a significant change. Few of the respondents were ready to leave their jobs in case of a serious conflict in the house, which shows that some women are still ready to sacrifice their careers if it is affecting their family responsibilities which shows that the double burden often acts as a barrier in the careers of women. Few of the respondents gave priority to their jobs, come what may they were not ready to compromise with their careers, that is an emerging trend.

Regarding husband's co-operation, the data shows that majority of the respondents' husbands were happy and even helped and encouraged them by sharing the children's responsibility; by doing housework, and by boosting their confidence and even by guiding them in their office problems, that is a significant change. Few of the respondents' husbands were not happy due to their wife's job as they felt that the respondent's job was affecting the children, their ego was hurt, and they felt that only if there is economic necessity, the wife should work, which shows that few men are still holding on to traditional attitudes regarding the employment of women.

The analysis on status of an economically independent woman to that of an economically dependent woman shows that, a majority of women accept the status of an economically independent woman as superior to that of an economically dependent woman and they feel that due to increasing prices, to maintain a lifestyle and for better future of the children double income has become necessary, that is an emerging trend. And some respondents felt that the status of an economically independent woman is equal to the status of an economically dependent woman, they were of the opinion that it is the husband's duty to earn for the house as it is the wife's duty to take care of the household duties which shows that there is no awareness among them about the benefits of economic independence. And this may be due to their illiteracy, early marriage and a limited world view.

The employed women's opinions on women's employment noticeably show that majority of the women favoured the idea that women should work to lead a better standard of life, for economic independence, for self-identity, financial security, self-satisfaction, to utilize one's time and education meaningfully. And few of the respondents felt that women should not work as it affects the family, children and moreover they have no emotional security, peace and leisure and they felt that they become overconfident, less feminine and also face harassment at workplace. These respondents felt that only under particular circumstances and if it is the wish of the family one should work. On the whole, it is seen that women want to be economically independent and have an individual identity.

The data collected from 91(23.1%) unemployed women on opposition to work shows that, still some women face opposition for doing a job either from parents, husband, or in-laws due to various reasons such as fear of neglecting the children and household responsibilities, family traditions, and fear of losing the status of the family. In case of unmarried respondents, it is the fear of not getting good marriage proposals for the daughters as taking up a job means interacting with men. Few of them were not able to complete their education due to early marriage and so were not qualified for a job. And few of the respondents were happy with their domestic duties and did not want to go for a job. So, in the end we can see that still some of them believe in old traditional attitudes with regard to women's employment.

Among the unemployed women, few of the respondents said that they would like to go for part-time jobs if given a chance as then they could make time for children, rest and recreation. Few of the respondents wanted full-time jobs as they were well-educated, and were in service before marriage but had given up their jobs due to husbands or in-laws opposition. Now, the children being grown up, they have ample time and felt idle and even repented for leaving their earlier jobs. Few of the respondents were ready to work from home as they felt that they were used to being at home and were not so confident about going out and working, moreover they could keep a watch on the house by working at home. While few of them felt that they were using their education for their children, to run the house properly and so they were happy to be housewives. In all, the data clearly shows that women's employment is still not free from the belief of traditional sex roles and employment of women is closely interwoven to her family and this builds her attitudes towards employment.

The data regarding opinion of unemployed respondents on woman's employment indicates that majority of the women held the opinion that women should work as it gives them economic independence, financial security, an identity, self-satisfaction and it leads to women's empowerment. This shows that most of the women are aware of the different facets of employment, that is a significant change. While few of the respondents were of the opinion that women should work only under special circumstances if necessary, as they felt that housework itself is a full-time job and one can use one's education to be a perfect homemaker, and going against the family's wish will disturb the peace of the house and moreover they felt that some needy person will be deprived of the job, which shows that some women are conservative in their outlook and are happy with their conventional roles.

The data regarding role of mass media shows that, more than half of the respondents under study read newspaper to get information on what is going on at national and international level and they felt that newspaper covers information from all four corners of the world and is affordable by all sections of society. Those who did not get time to get into the details of a newspaper watched TV to know about what's happening around the world. In all it can be said that the respondents are interested in knowing about the going-ons all over the world, that is a significant change.

Almost all the respondents watched TV regularly for news, for health knowledge, for cookery shows, comedy shows and serials.

Some of the respondents felt that comedy serials are relaxing; some felt that serials are boring and irrelevant and spoil children. One respondent felt that one should know how to select proper channel for watching instead of blaming the media. And some even felt that everything depends on the angle of viewing.

The analysis on the impact of TV programmes shows that nearly half of the respondents felt that TV does not help in liberating women from the shackles of customs and felt that women should be presented as having her own identity, but they are still shown in traditional roles.

The majority of the respondents felt that TV helped one in acquiring knowledge by watching channels such as discovery channel, history channel and so on and they also said that even serials and advertisements are educative. While some felt that TV is not helping in acquisition of knowledge and programmes such as reality shows are affecting children's confidence levels.

Almost all the respondents agreed that the TV was helping in the knowledge of national and international events and they felt that even an illiterate can get knowledge of the events. It shows that women are interested in knowing about national and international events and also because it has no literacy barrier.

The above data shows that majority of the respondents agreed that TV was useful in development of educational knowledge and they said that it depend on the viewer to watch meaningful channels and they also felt that parents should cultivate the habit of watching educational channels in children. Some of the respondents felt that TV does not help in development of educational knowledge, they felt that today children watch cartoon channels most of the time, so these respondents suggested that the channels watched by children should be presented in an informative and educative way.

Majority of the respondents felt that TV helped in the development of health knowledge; as certain channels focused on health topics and they also said that advertisements on various diseases shown were educative and informative. While some of the respondents felt that TV is not useful in development of health knowledge as a doctor's advice was necessary for any illness and to carry out the exercises shown on TV could mislead and confuse the viewers.

The data indicates that more than half of the respondents agreed that TV has been useful in removal of caste consciousness and nowadays class determined one's status and not caste at least in the cities and also the number of inter-caste and inter-religious marriages is on the rise. Some of the respondents felt that though the change is evident in cities, inter-caste marriages are not allowed and caste wars take place, in rural areas and villages and even cities experience caste riots. They suggested that the government should do more to create awareness among the people as it controls a section of mass media.

Nearly half of the respondents held the view that TV helped in eradication of the dowry custom as some serials dealt with the curse of dowry system and encouraged young girls to stand up against the custom of dowry. Some of the respondents felt that TV played no role in removal of dowry custom; and showed meaningless serials. They felt that the media should concentrate more on social problems present in the society to change the mindsets of people.

The data on watching movies shows that almost all the respondents watched movies and most of them liked to watch family-oriented or educational movies with a social message which is a promising change. The youngsters liked to watch romantic and suspense movies as they were exciting while the older women liked to watch old movies as they felt that such movies were comforting and soothing to the eyes and ears. Few of the respondents were not interested in seeing movies and they also felt that today's movies were not worth watching.

Data regarding use of computers by the respondents shows that nearly half of the respondents used the computers for various purposes as getting information, for storing data, for communication purposes, they felt that computers are faster and have made the work easier but as it is a machinery they felt that one should always maintain written records also to be on the safe side. Some felt that due to the internet, students are forgetting the significance of reading books as they can download any information directly from the net which they felt is not a good habit. While more than half of the respondents did not use computers as they had no knowledge of it or they had no facility or they did not need it.

As for data regarding political issues, it is seen that almost all women under study participated in voting as they felt that each vote counts as it decides the destiny of a party, that is a significant change from the traditional days. Some of the respondents did not vote due to change of address and while in the process of getting their names included in the new list, few of the respondents' names were not in the voter's list and few of the respondents were indifferent and did not vote as they felt that all political parties had their own selfish motives and it did not matter who won.

It is seen that almost all the respondents did not consult anyone on whom to vote and exercised their vote independently which shows that the respondents' political awareness has increased and it can said to be a noteworthy change. But few of the respondents voted according to their husband's wish, which shows that some of them are still stuck up in conventional values and few of the respondents discussed with their friends or relatives before casting their votes.

The data on campaigning activities shows that some of the respondents took part in canvassing, they distributed slips, pamphlets during elections, shouted slogans and moreover they also took part in 'padyatras'. The four respondents who were from political background and were members of political parties took part in political meetings and arranged meetings to give knowledge to the people about their rights. They also took part in agitations to put forth their demands, to show their unity and support to their leader, and to bring a change in society. One attention-grabbing finding is that though almost all the respondents exercised their voting rights, when it came to actual participation in politics they were not interested in campaigning activities as they felt that politics was a dirty field and not meant for women and it harmed the status of the family. They were of the opinion that there are other ways of serving the nation. On the whole, it can be said that though women voters are increasing in number but they are still traditional in outlook when it comes to active participation in politics. It seems household tasks, restrictions imposed by the family members on women's movement and lack of interest are the hurdles in their path of participation.

Data regarding 33 per cent reservation for women reveals that almost all the respondents held the opinion that there should be 33 per cent reservation for women in legislative bodies as the reservation bill will be a means of women's empowerment and development. While some of the respondents felt that there should not be 33 per cent reservation for women in legislative bodies as they feel women should come in politics based on their capabilities as in other fields, and by asking reservation women are agreeing that they are inferior. They said that women representatives remain as puppets whereas the main decision-makers are men and moreover due to controversies involved women think that politics is a dirty field. They suggested that the government and the legal system should work to change the opinion of people regarding politics. Some felt that irrespective of sex, a sincere and devoted person should be at the decision-making level, as with power even some women become selfish.

Data on membership to organizations indicates that very few of the respondents were members of some associations such as *mahila mandals, bhajan mandals, bal sansthas*, labour unions and doctor's associations which worked for economic upliftment of women by giving loans on low interest rates, welfare of children, organized free check-ups for the poor, some were involved in religious activities. The respondents helped these organizations by teaching and guiding the poor children, by counselling the women on various issues, by updating them on the legalities in case of a problem, by arranging lectures on health-related topics, by organizing free check-ups and by organizing 'satsangs' and visits to religious places. While some were members of political party, two of them were corporators and they solved the ordinary man's problems by taking them to the higher authority and two of them were members who helped their parties by organizing meetings, by campaigning during elections and by creating political awareness among the people. Thus, it is seen that women's participation in organizations is very limited. It seems that the women's societal and political life is still ruled by tradition and family obligations, though it has started it will take time to gather impetus.

Majority of the respondents were of the opinion that increased women's participation in politics will bring qualitative change in administration, they felt that due to qualities such as understanding, affection, patience and sensitiveness in handling problems, women can be good leaders and with more women in politics, women's problems will be solved, the status of women will rise and will lead to development of the nation. While some of the respondents felt that before elections irrespective of gender the candidates make false promises never to be fulfilled, once they are in power they become selfish. They also said that when a woman enters politics she is a mere puppet and the main decision-makers are men, so politics is not the field for women. According to some, the nation's welfare is dependent on individuals with ethics, morals and commitment to work rather than a bunch of politicians. In a nutshell, it can be said that women are interested in politics but when it comes to actual participation, due to traditional values on one hand and due to increasing corruption, criminalization and muscle power in politics on the other hand, women are uncertain about their success.

Hence, it is seen in the present study that the women by the attainment of education and better economic status were found to be developing new and different attitudes and opinions. They have started questioning the traditional image of women and are trying to come out of the image of submissive women by asserting their rights through participation in the decision-making process in the family, by showing negative attitude towards some traditional customs, beliefs, practices and duties towards the husband in Indian society, having a positive attitude towards role fluidity between husband and wife or male and female, having a positive attitude towards education, employment, economic independence, political participation and so on. In all, in the present study an overall change is seen in the position of women and she is in the process of development though it may be slow.

Bibliography

Adams, M. 1972, "The Single Women in Today's Society: A Reappraisal", in H. Wortis and C. Rabinowitz (eds.), *The Women's Movement: Social and Psychological Lifestyles*. New York: AMS Press.

——. 1976, *Single Blessedness: Observations on the Single Status in Married Society*. New York: Basic Books.

Ahuja, Ram. 1994, *Indian Social System*. Jaipur and New Delhi: Rawat Publications.

Altekar, A.S. 1962, *The Position of Women in Hindu Civilization*. Delhi: Motilal Banarsidass.

Baker, L.G. 1973, "The Personal and Social Adjustment of Never Married Woman", *Journal of Marriage and Family*, 30, 473–79.

Behura, N.K. and R.P. Mohanty. 2005, *Status and Empowerment of the Girl Child*. New Delhi: Discovery Publishing House.

Boserup, E. 1970, *Women's Role in Economic Development*. New York: St. Martin's Press.

Bossard, James H.S. 1954, *The Sociology of Child Development*. New York: Harper, 282–86.

Braito, R. and D. Anderson. 1983, "The Ever-Single Elderly Woman", in E.W. Markson (ed.), *Older Women: Issues and Prospects*. Lexington, MA: Lexington Books.

Census of India. 1981 (Series-I, India) Part-II Special, Delhi.

Cormack, Margaret. 1961, *The Hindu Women*. Bombay: Asia Publishing House, 178.

——. 1969, *She Who Rides a Peacock*. New York: Praeger.

Dak, T.M. 1988, *Women and Work in Indian Society*. Delhi: Discovery Publishing House.

Desai, I.P. 1953, *High School Students in Pune*. Poona: Deccan College.

Desai, Neera. 1957, *Women in Modern India*. Bombay: Vora Publishers.

Dube, S.C. 1963, "Men's and Women's Role in India", in Barbara E. Ward (ed.), *Women in the New Asia*. Paris: UNESCO.

Feldman, F.L. 1958, *Work in the Lives of Married Women*. National Manpower Council, New York: Columbia University Press, p. 94.

Gerth, H.H. and C.W. Mills (eds.), 1946, *Max Weber: Essays in Sociology*. New York: Oxford University Press, p. 180.

Gore, M.S. 1968, *Urbanization and Family Change*. Bombay: Popular Prakashan.

Government of India. 1964, "International Trends", Women in Employment. Labour Bureau, Ministry of Labour and Employment, 58–59.

——. 1974, *Report of the Committee on the Status of Women in India*. New Delhi.

Gupta, Giri Raj. 1976, *Family and Social Change in Modern India*. Delhi: Vikas Publishing House.

Hand, H.B. 1957, "Working Mothers and Maladjusted Children", in *Journal of Educational Sociology*, January 30.

Hate, C.A. 1930, The Socio-Economic Conditions of Educated Women in Bombay City. Study prepared in the University School of Economics and Sociology, Bombay.

——. 1969, *Changing Status of Woman in Post-Independence India*. Bombay: Allied Publishers Pvt. Ltd., p. 66.

Herald 14 February 1997, 'Only 7% Parliamentarians World-wide headed by Women'.

Hooja, S.L. 1969, *Dowry System in India: A Case Study*. New Delhi: Asia Press.

Immanuel, M. 1998, *Women and Development*. Ahmedabad: Karnavati Publications.

Indra, M.A. 1940, *The Status of Women in Ancient India*. Anarkali: Minerva Bookshop.

Jayal, Shakambari. 1966, *The Status of Women in the Epics*. Delhi: Motilal Banarsidass.

Jena, Sanjay K. 1994, *Working Women and Modernization*. Delhi: Ashish Publishing House.

Joshi, Rama J. 1973, "Contemporary Change in the Socio-Economic Role of Women in India: Its Impact on Family Life", in Kamala Bhasin (ed.), *The Position of Women in India*. Bombay: Leslie Swahney Programme of Training for Democracy.

Kapadia, K.M. 1959, "The Family in Transition", *Sociological Bulletin*, Vol. 8, No. 2, September.

——. 1966, *Marriage and Family in India*. Bombay: Oxford University Press.

Kapur, Promilla. 1970, *Marriage and Working Women in India*. Delhi: Vikas Publications.

——. 1973, *Love, Marriage and Sex*. Delhi: Vikas Publishing House.

——. 1974, *The Changing Status of Working Women in India*. Delhi: Vikas Publishing House Pvt. Ltd.

Karakal, Malini. 1991, "Abortion Laws and Abortion Situation in India", *Issues in Reproductive and Genetic Engineering*, Vols. 3 and 4.

Karve, I. 1953, *Kinship Organization in India*. Bombay: Asia Publishing House.

Kaur, Inderjeet. 1983, *Status of Hindu Women in India*. Delhi: Chugh Publication.

Klein, Voila. 1965, *Britain's Married Women Workers*. London: Routledge and Kegan Paul.

Krishnan, Prabha, Anitha Dighe and Purnima Rao. 1986, Affirmation and Denial: Sex Role Patterns on Doordarshan. Paper presented at IAMCR Conference, New Delhi.

Kumari, Pratima. 1988, *Changing Values among Young Women*. Delhi: Amar Prakashan.

Kuppuswamy, B. 1981, *Social Change in India*. New Delhi: Vikas Publishing House Pvt. Ltd.

Kurane, Anjali. 2005, "Socio-Economic Development among the Warlis in Maharashtra", in *Dimensions of Researches in Indian Anthropology*. Oriental Anthropologist Series, Vol. II.

——. 2006, "Development through Watershed: A Study of Two Villages of Ahmednagar District", in *Empowering Rural India: Experiments and Experiences*. New Delhi: Kanishka Publishers, 107–23.

Lalneihzovi. 2007, *Women's Development in India: Problems and Prospects*. New Delhi: Mittal Publications.

Lerner, Daniel. 1967, "International Cooperation and Communication in National Development", in Daniel Lerner and Wilbur Schramm (eds.).

Lundberg, Ferdinand and Marynia F. Farnham. 1947, *Modern Women: The Lost Sex*. New York: Harper, as quoted in the Employed Mother, 7.

Madan, T.N. 1976, "The Hindu Women at Home", in B.R. Nanda (ed.), *Indian Women*. New Delhi: Vikas.

Mehta, Hansa. 1981, *Indian Women*. Delhi: Butala and Company.

Mehta, Vatsala. 1956, The Hindu Widow (With Special Reference To Gujarat). Thesis submitted for M.A. degree in the Dept. of Sociology, University of Bombay.

Misra, R.P. 1985, *Development Issues of Our Times*. New Delhi: Concept Publishing House.

Murdock, George P. 1949, *Social Structure*. New York: Macmillan, p. 8.

Nagendra, Shailaja. 2007, *Issues in Women Education and Empowerment*. Jaipur: ABD Publishers.

National Family. 1998–99, as available in Women and Men, 2000, Health Survey-II, Ministry of PPI, Government of India.

——. 1999, International Institute of Population Sciences, Health Survey (NHFS-II) Mumbai.

Nye, F. Ivan. 1952, "Adolescent-Parent Adjustment", in *Marriage and Family Living* 14, November.

——. 1958, *Family Relationships and Delinquent Behaviour*. New York: John Wiley and Sons, Inc.

——. 1959, "Employment Status of Mothers and Adjustment of Adolescent Children", *Marriage and Family Living*, Vol. 21, August, 240–44.

Oakley, Ann. 1974, *Housewife*. London: Allen Dave.

Pandya, Rameshwari. 2008, *Women in Changing India*. New Delhi: Serials Publications.

Parsons, Talcott and Robert F. Bales. 1955, *Family, Socialization and Interaction Process*. Glencoe, III: Free Press.

Parvin, M. Razia. 2005, *Empowerment of Women: Strategies and Systems for Gender Justice*. New Delhi: Dominant Publishers.

Ramanamma, A. 1979, *Graduate Employed Women in an Urban Setting*. Poona: Dastane Ramchandra and Company.

Ranade, S.N. and P. Ramchandra. 1964, *Attitudes of Women to Part-Time Employment*. Bombay: Tata Institute of Social Research.

Rani, Kala. 1976, *Role Conflict in Working Women*. New Delhi: Chetna Publications.

Rao, V.V. Prakasha and V. Nandini Rao. 1982, *Marriage, Family and Women in India*. New Delhi: Heritage Publishers.

Robson, Colin. 2007, *How to do a Research*. Oxford, UK: Blackwell Publishing.

Saini, Shiv Kumar. 1980, *Development of Education in India*. New Delhi: Cosmo Publications, 13–14.

Sengupta, Padmini. 1974, *Story of Women of India*. New Delhi: Indian Book Company.

Seth, Mira. 2001, *Women and Development*. New Delhi: Sage Publications.

Sethi, Raj Mohini. 1976, *Modernization of Working Women in Developing Societies*. New Delhi: National Publishing House.

Shahida and Lalitha K. Sami. 2007, *Indian Women in Development Perspective*. New Delhi: Anmol Publications.

Sharma, B.A.V., D. Ravindra Prasad and P. Satyanarayana. 1985, *Research Methods in Social Sciences*. New Delhi: Sterling Publishers.

Sharma, K.L. 2007, *Indian Social Structure and Change*. Jaipur: Rawat Publications.

Shirwadkar, Meena. 1979, *Image of Indian Women in the Indo-Anglican Novel*. New Delhi: Sterling Publishers.

Siegel, Alberta E. and Lois M. Stolz. 1959, *Dependence and Independence in the Children of Working Mother*.

Soni, Jasprit Kaur. 2006, *Women Empowerment: Exploring the Facts*. Delhi: Authors Press.

Stein, P. 1978, "The Lifestyles and Life Changes of the Never-Married", in *Marriage and Family Review*, July/August, 1–11.

Sunday Times of India. Pune, October 14, 2007.

Sur, A.K. 1973, *Sex and Marriage in India*. Bombay: Allied Publishers.

Talwar, Usha. 1984, *Social Profile of Working Women*. Jodhpur: Jain Brothers.

Thakur, B.S. and Binod C. Agrawal. 2004, *Media Utilization for the Development of Women and Children*. New Delhi: Concept Publishing House.

The Times of India. Pune, September 29, 2007.

Thomas, P. 1964, *Indian Women through the Ages*. Bombay: Asia Publishing House, p. 306.

Widge, N.K. and R. Nag. 1989, "National Efforts for the Development of Women and Children", in B.S. Thakur and Binod C. Agrawal (eds.), *Media Utilization for the Development of Women and Children*. New Delhi: Concept Publishing House.

Youssef, N. 1974, Women and Work in Developing Societies. Population Monograph Series No. 15, Berkeley: University of California Institute of International Studies.

Index

Adams, M., 64
Ahuja, Ram, 3, 49, 79
Altekar, A.S., 42, 43, 96

Baker, L.G., 64
Behura, N.K. and Mohanty, R.P., 48
Benoist, A.D., 14
Boserup, E., 114
Bossard, James H.S., 135, 141
Braito, R. and Anderson, D., 64

Chatterjee, Meera, 8
Committee on the Status of Women, 96, 158
communication revolution, 12
Cormack, Margaret, 55, 149

Dak, T.M., 74
decision-making, 25
  among married women, 28–54
  among unmarried women, 54–71
  among women, 25–27
Desai, Neera, 39, 133
development, 1, 2
  aim of, 1
  concept of, 1, 2, 3
  definition of, 1, 2
  designing for, 3
  nature of, 1
  process of, 1
Dube, S.C., 79, 80

economic empowerment of women, 10, 16, 114
education
  process of, 9
  role of, in improving women's status, 9, 15–16, 102

Feldman, F.L., 131
female political participation, 13
  in India, 13–14, 168
female work participation
  in India, 11–12

Gore, M.S., 60, 137
Gupta, Giri Raj, 35

Hand, H.B., 124
Hate, C.A., 38, 67, 149, 168, 177
Hewlett, Sylvia, 124
Hooja, S.L., 40

Indian society, 6, 37
  customs/practices in, 37,
    seeking women's opinion
    regarding, 37–50
  women's status in, 6–9, 9–10, 26
Indra, M.A., 68
Ivan Nye, F., 124, 139

Jain, Shashi, 165, 169, 171
Jayal Shakumbari, 68
Jena, Sanjay Ketan, 78, 169
Joshi, Rama J., 27

Kapadia, K.M., 39, 60, 133
Kapur, Promilla, 43, 66, 68, 69, 133
Karakal, Malini, 8
Karve, Iravati, 26
Kaur, Inderjeet, 99, 102, 169
Klien, Voila, 117
Krishnan, Prabha et al., 153
Kumari, Pratima, 69, 98, 150, 165
Kumari, Preeti, 151, 155, 156, 158,
    159, 160
Kuppuswamy, B., 150
Kurane, Anjali, 2

Lerner, Daniel, 150, 166
Lundberg, F. and Farnham, M.F.,
    135, 141

Madan, T.N., 33
Mahajan, Kamlesh, 153
mass media, 149
  as the mobile multiplier, 150
  means of, 150
  role of, 150, in women's
    development, 150–67
  women's exposure to, 151–67
Mehta, Hansa, 96
Mehta, Vatsala, 43
Misra, R.P., 2
Murdock, George P., 26

Nehru, Jawaharlal, 10

Oakley, Ann, 74

paraya dhan
  concept of, 7, 9, 90
Parsons, Talcott and Bales, Robert
    F., 141
Parvin, M. Razia, 4
'pativrata'
  concept of, 7
political empowerment
  of women, 13
political participation
  concept of, 168
power, 26
Prakasha Rao, V.V. and Nandini
    Rao, V., 97
property rights
  of women, 90, women's attitude
  towards, 91–93
Pune, 18, 197

Ramanamma, A., 15
Ranade, S.N. and Ramchandra, P.,
    117
Rani, Kala, 33
Reddy, Raghunanda, 69

role fluidity
  between husband and wife, 73–90

Saini, Shiv Kumar, 10
Salgoankar, Seema, 17, 171, 172, 174, 177
Sami, Lalitha K. and Shahida, 3, 11
Second Sex, 194
Sen, Amartya, 3
Sengupta, Padmini, 4
Seth, Mira, 11, 16, 115, 160
Sethi, Mohini, 97
Sharma, K.L., 38, 41
Shirwadkar, Meena, 97
Siegel, Alberta E. and Stolz, Lois M., 124
social participation/life
  women's attitude towards, 50–54
Soni, Jasprit Kaur, 10, 14, 15
Sur, A.K., 41, 68

Talwar, Usha, 66
Thomas, P., 4
TV
  impact of, on women, 154

Vidyarthi, L.P., 2
Vivekananda, Swami, 5

Weber, Max, 26
Weiner, Myron, 168
Widge, M.K. and Nag, R., 16
women's development, 3
  in India, historical perspective of, 3–5
  issues involved in, 6,
    socio-cultural, 6–9, 25–94,
    educational, 9–10, 95–113
    economic, 10–13, 113–43
    political, 13–14, 168–82
  role of media in, 12–13, 16, 149–67
women's education
  in India, history of, 95–96; in the post-independence period, 96–97; reasons for slow growth, 96–97; women's perspective on, 95–113
women's status, 3
  in Indian society, 6–9, 10–11, 114

Youssef, N., 114